讀莊子聞朱晦菴郎世

按上數編書非莊即老會說忘言始知道
萬言千句不自能忘堪笑今朝梅雨霽青
天好　一壑一丘輕衫短帽白髮多時故
人少子雲何在應有玄經遺草江河流日
夜何時了

TWAYNE'S WORLD AUTHORS SERIES

A Survey of the World's Literature

Sylvia E. Bowman, Indiana University

GENERAL EDITOR

CHINA

Howard S. Levy, Tokyo
and
William R. Schultz, University of Arizona

EDITORS

Hsin Ch'i- hi

(TWAS 169)

TWAYNE'S WORLD AUTHORS SERIES (TWAS)

The purpose of TWAS is to survey the major writers —novelists, dramatists, historians, poets, philosophers, and critics—of the nations of the world. Among the national literatures covered are those of Australia, Canada, China, Eastern Europe, France, Germany, Greece, India, Italy, Japan, Latin America, New Zealand, Poland, Russia, Scandinavia, Spain and the African nations, as well as Hebrew, Yiddish, and Latin Classical literatures. This survey is complemented by Twayne's United States Authors Series and English Authors Series.

The intent of each volume in these series is to present a critical-analytical study of the works of the writer; to include biographical and historical material that may be necessary for understanding, appreciation, and critical appraisal of the writer; and to present all material in clear, concise English—but not to vitiate the scholarly content of the work by doing so.

Hsin Ch'i-chi

By IRVING YUCHENG LO

Indiana University

TWAYNE PUBLISHERS, INC. :: NEW YORK

Dedicated to

MADELEINE DORAN

*Ruth C. Wallerstein Professor
of English Literature*

The University of Wisconsin

Acknowledgments

For permission to use excerpts of published works, I wish to express my gratitude to the following:

Chilmark Press, Inc. for material from *The Anathémata* by David Jones. Issued in 1965 by the Viking Press, Inc.

The Clarendon Press, Oxford, for material from *Ch'u Tz'u: The Songs of the South* by David Hawkes. © 1959 by Oxford University Press.

Farrar, Straus, and Giroux, Inc. for excerpts from *On Poetry and Poets* by T. S. Eliot. Copyright © 1943, 1945, 1951, 1954, 1956, 1957 by T. S. Eliot.

Harcourt, Brace & World, Inc. for excerpts from *Selected Essays, 1917–1932* by T. S. Eliot. Copyright 1932, 1936, 1950, by Harcourt, Brace and World, Inc.; copyright, 1960, 1964, by T. S. Eliot.

Indiana University Press for the use of some of my own translations of Hsin Ch'i-chi published in the first volume of *K'uei Hsing*. Copyright © 1971 by Indiana University Press.

James J. Y. Liu and The University of Chicago Press for material from *The Art of Chinese Poetry* © 1962 by James J. Y. Liu. Published 1962. Second Impression 1966. First Phoenix Edition 1966. Printed in the United States of America. *The Chinese Knight-Errant* © 1967 by James J. Y. Liu. Published 1967. Composed and Printed in England. *The Poetry of Li Shang-yin* © 1969 by James J. Y. Liu. All rights reserved. Published 1969. Printed in the United States of America.

The Macmillan Company for lines from "Lapis Lazuli" from *Collected Poems* of William Butler Yeats. Copyright 1940 by Georgie Yeats, renewed 1968 by Bertha Georgie Yeats.

Random House, Inc. for excerpts from *The Dyer's Hand and Other Essays* by W. H. Auden. Copyright 1948, 1950, 1952, 1953, 1954; © 1956, 1957, 1958, 1960, 1962.

The University of Wisconsin Press for translations of T'ao Ch'ien's poems by James R. Hightower published in *Wen-lin: Studies in the Chinese Humanities,* edited by Chow Tse-tsung. © 1958 by the Regents of the University of Wisconsin.

Burton Watson and the Columbia University Press for portions reprinted from *The Complete Works of Chuang Tzu,* translated by Burton Watson. Copyright © 1968 Columbia University Press.

Explanation of Romanization Rules and Other Symbols Used

1. All Chinese words, names, and titles are romanized according to the modified Wade-Giles system. (Omitted are the circumflex above the *e* and the breve above the *u* in *ssu, tzu,* and *tz'u.*)

2. Geographical names are given in the forms as they are known today, except for their first occurrence in the text. In such cases, the modern name appears inside the parentheses; thus "Lin-an (Hangchow)" refers to the city of Hangchow, known as Lin-an in Sung times.

3. Translations of Chinese official ranks and titles follow E. Kracke, *Translations of Sung Civil Service Titles* (Paris, 1957).

4. References to a Chinese text, unless it is a modern edition, have been simplified and details of publication generally omitted; the numeral to the left of a virgule indicates the *chüan* (Chinese "volume") number, and that to the right indicates the page number, with "a" and "b" referring to the recto and the verso page.

5. The Selected Bibliography will include only those books most relevant to the study of Hsin Ch'i-chi, but not all of the "frequently cited works" mentioned in the Notes, since the indication of editions used has already been included in the Notes. A separate list of these titles would be of inordinate length and of no use to nonspecialists.

Preface

Classical Chinese poetry is written in many forms and many styles, developing from an old tradition and continuing to evolve new modes of composition until the fourteenth century. The heavy weight of tradition is felt by all artists in China; and yet a poet, if he is a creative genius, is frequently able to break away from the forces of traditionalism and achieve a distinctive style of his own. The poetry of this order is certainly the product of individual talent; it is also a product of the various kinds of tension in the poet's own age resulting from social and political realities to be reckoned with, or from changing taste in esthetics and literature, or from new directions of intellectual inquiry. The greater the tension, the finer the product. "Art never improves," Eliot says, but "the material of art is never quite the same."

This book is planned to introduce to the English-speaking audience the poetry written in the "Lyric Meter" (known as *tz'u* in Chinese) by Hsin Ch'i-chi, a poet of the Southern Sung dynasty (1127–1279) —a period of division in China and also a time of great creativity in literature, philosophy, and the arts. Conscious of the importance of a poet's *milieu* (linguistic as well as nonlinguistic) to a full appreciation of his work, I have attempted to consider Hsin's work in the context of older traditions and in the light of Hsin's individual contribution to Chinese poetry. Toward this aim, I have also provided accurate translations of thirty-nine of his lyrics, transliterations of the Chinese text for some, and full annotation for all the poems I have translated.

Hsin Ch'i-chi (1140–1207), better known to Chinese readers by his courtesy-name of Hsin Chia-hsüan, is admired no less for his poetic accomplishment than for the life and philosophy embodied in his works. Born in Shantung thirteen years after the collapse of the Northern Sung dynasty at the hands of the Jurchëd (or Nü-chen) tribe, he spent nearly all of his adult life in South China, first as a soldier fighting against the northern Chin empire, then as an official, and finally as a recluse. Because he felt so intensely the troubles of his time, his poetry often expresses strong patriotic, or heroic, sentiments. Therefore, he has been commonly referred to as China's "patriotic poet," which in a real sense means "national poet."

Among Chinese critics and literary historians, Hsin Ch'i-chi is widely acknowledged as a major *tz'u* writer; that is to say, a poet in the "lyric mode of composition"—a fame he earned not only because he was the most prolific among those who wrote in the Lyric Meter (over six hundred poems), but also because he was among the most genuine and the most erudite of all Chinese poets. (Occasionally I have used the word "lyricist" to refer to a *"tz'u* writer," although I am aware of the inadequacy of this translation because of the restricted connotation of this word as compared to "poet." For some inexplicable reason, Chinese critics like to differentiate between a "poet" (*shih-jen*) and a *"tz'u* writer" (*tz'u-jen*); but if one accepts the argument that *tz'u* is a subgenre of *shih* (see Chapter 2), then a *tz'u* writer is a poet. I do not make any distinction between the two terms; where I use the word "lyricist" in this book, I mean "poet," or one who writes in the Lyric Meter.) Particularly admired is the remarkably wide range of his style: from earthy humor and colloquialism to high reaches of philosophical speculation and the fecundity of his learning, from moods of the deepest melancholy and tenderness to the most spirited outbursts of high-minded sentiments. Like China's recluse-poet T'ao Ch'ien (T'ao Yüan-ming, 365–427) of another era, whom he intensely admired, Hsin also showed a rare sensitivity to nature; and in his lyrics he attempted to answer life's problems with lessons he drew as readily from nature as from history or philosophy.

Hsin's reputation among Chinese intellectuals of the modern period is especially high. Scholars since the Republican era, beginning with Liang Ch'i-ch'ao (1873–1929) and Wang Kuo-wei (1877–1927), have contributed much to our understanding of the poet's life and work. As the appreciation of poetry transcends differences in political beliefs (such as those presently dividing China), the current interest in Hsin Ch'i-chi is manifested in the publication, between 1946 and 1964, in three capitals of China—Chungking, Peking, and Taipei (see Bibliography)—of six biographies of the poet. As a full vindication of Hsin's poetic genius, it could be pointed out that Hsin, the most allusive of the lyricists, was called "the first among major *tz'u* writers" by none other than Hu Shih (1891–1962), the apostle of the New Culture Movement in China, during the late 1920's, even though he had denounced the use of allusions (for allusions' sake) in his advocacy of the use of the vernacular speech in literature.

I have devoted the first chapter of this book to giving an account of the poet's life and of the political and social background of his time. In the second chapter, I have attempted to describe the historical origin of this poetic subgenre known as *tz'u,* along with its most salient characteristics, but without intending to give a complete history of Chinese poetry. In Chapter 5, the discussion of the technical aspects of *tz'u* composition is resumed, concentrating on Hsin's mastery of the various techniques and conventions, under the title of "The Poet as Craftsman." Chapters 3, 4, and 6 contain an analysis of the many styles of Hsin's lyrics, shown in his patriotic or "heroic" poems, in his nature poems, and in his philosophical poems. Chapters 3 through 6 will also contain my translations of Hsin's poems (which are consecutively numbered 1–39, except for isolated passages). Allusions found in his lyrics will be explained in the "Notes to the Poems" section. Unless otherwise noted, all translations from Chinese sources used in this book, including the works of other poets, are my own.

In my translations, I aim at preserving as much of the meaning and the flavor of the original as it is possible for me to do in English. I have done very little paraphrasing, except at places where I feel there is absolute need; and such departures, when they occur, will be pointed out in the Notes. Even in the matter of word order, I have tried to stay close to the original text. On the other hand, I recognize that differences in the structure of the two languages—English and Chinese—do exist, with the latter being noninflectional and highly connotative. Therefore, a translator must on occasion take certain liberties if he wishes to avoid the risk of writing pidgin English. For instance, the first-person pronoun "I," as the subject of a sentence, is rarely given in a line of Chinese verse but can be inferred from the context. Such pronouns, along with English prepositions wherever they are needed, will be provided. Measure words, as well as names of birds and flowers, can only be approximations or the nearest equivalents. (The word *li,* meaning "a Chinese mile," equivalent to approximately one-third of an English mile, has been so converted only when the actual distance of a place is being referred to; otherwise *li* is either left as a transliterated word or translated simply as "mile.") In other words, what I hope to achieve is to cast the original poem in an English idiom and in a rhythm that will be both pleasing to the ear and appropriate to the sense.

In the matter of form, I follow the line lengths of the original faithfully, in order to illustrate and preserve the *enjambment* feature of *tz'u,* which is a departure from the traditional form of poetry (*shih*)—*tz'u* being alternatively known in Chinese as the "long-and-short verse" (*ch'ang-tuan-chü*). I have numbered the lines also according to the original, including those that mark only a "pause" (*tou*). Capital letters are used at the beginning of each of the verse lines counted in this manner. I do not use rhyme in my translation except when the rhyming occurs naturally; nor have I tried every time to reproduce in English such poetic devices found in the original as onomatopoeia, the use of reduplicatives, and alliteration.

Translations of poetry, as James J. Y. Liu has written, "are only compromises, between two different ways of thinking and feeling." As such, they have not been fortunate enough to engage the attention of all serious scholars, but have been all too often left, so to speak, to be "farmed" out to amateurs. In my mind, a "compromise" is always something challenging and rewarding when it *can* be worked out. But when it leads to a greater understanding of something else, as it is intended to do, it will be that much more rewarding. The late William Riley Parker, speaking of Greek and Roman classics in translation, has remarked that the reading of translations is "like being kissed through a veil—exciting contact, no doubt, if one has never been kissed directly." Naturally, the sooner this veil is lifted, the happier will be the result for both parties.

I wish to acknowledge with gratitude a Fulbright-Hays Senior Faculty grant made by the U.S. Office of Education, which enabled me to spend a year in the Far East, when I did the bulk of the research. I also owe a special debt of gratitude to Professor Cheng Ch'ien of National Taiwan University for making available to me the results of his own research on Hsin Ch'i-chi, including his unpublished manuscript of an annotated edition of Hsin's lyrics; and to my friend and teacher, Mr. S. N. Yüan of Taipei, Taiwan, for his encouragement and help.

I also wish to acknowledge a special debt to several of my friends and colleagues in the United States: to Professors C. T. Hsia, of Columbia University; James J. Y. Liu, of Stanford University; William R. Schultz, of the University of Arizona, editor of the Chinese section of the Twayne World Authors Series, and Kenneth Yasuda, of Indiana University, for having read the rough draft of my translation of a number of the poems included in this book and offered their criticism, or for answering certain queries. To Professor Y. T. Wang, of the University of Pittsburgh, for having read Chapter 1 of this book in its first draft and offered me his help; to Professor Richard Mather, of the University of Minnesota, for answering queries related to *Shih-shuo hsin-yü*; to Professor T. H. Tsien, of the Far Eastern Library, University of Chicago; to Dr. K. T. Wu, of the Library of Congress; and to Mr. and Mrs. Lucian Wu of Washington, D.C., for their personal kindnesses; to Professor Edward Callan, of Western Michigan University, for his special insight into modern poetry and poetics. And to Mr. C. H. Wang, University of Massachusetts, for his research assistance.

I also wish to acknowledge a pleasant debt to three of my former students in a seminar on Chinese poetry, at Indiana University, who have benefited me with their criticism of some of the translations used in this book when they were first read in the class: Messieurs Eugene C. Eoyang, now a member of the faculty at Indiana University, Department of Comparative Literature; Jerome Seaton, now on the faculty of the University of North Carolina; and Michael Workman. I appreciate especially the help of Mr. Eoyang who read the manuscript in its final form and made many invaluable editorial suggestions.

I owe a large debt of gratitude to Professor Wu-chi Liu of my own department for having read the entire manuscript in its first draft and rendered me help on numerous occasions. Without his astute criticism, this book could never have taken its present shape as painlessly for me as it did. I am grateful to my wife, Lena, for the preparation of the typescript which received her professional editorial attention.

IRVING YUCHENG LO

Indiana University

Contents

Translation of the Lyrics

Chronology

1140   May 28 (11th day of the 5th lunar month) Hsin Ch'i-chi born in Li-ch'eng (modern Tsinan, Shantung province).

1161   Joined the anti-Jurchëd expedition led by Ken Ching; moved South.

1162   Granted audience with Emperor Kao-tsung at Chien-k'ang (modern Nanking), appointed Junior Secretary; killed Chang An-kuo, the assassin of Ken Ching; appointed Signatory Official to the prefectural staff of Chiang-yin (in modern Kiangsu province).

1165   Presented to the throne "The Humble Offering of Ten Discourses."

1168   Appointed Signatory Official to the prefectural staff at Nanking.

1170   Granted second audience with Kao-tsung; presented to the Prime Minister Yü Yün-wen the "Nine Treatises."

1171   Appointed to the Ministry of Agriculture.

1172   Appointed Magistrate of Ch'u-chou (in modern Anhwei province).

1174   Recommended by Prime Minister Yeh Heng and summoned for an audience with Emperor Hsiao-tsung; appointed to the Ministry of Grains.

1175   Sent to suppress insurrections led by the tea-merchant rebel Lai Wen-cheng, in Hupeh, Hunan, and Kiangsi; appointed Judicial Intendant of Kiangsi; appointed Compiler of Imperial Archives.

1177   Appointed Magistrate of Chiang-ling (in modern Hupeh province) and Pacification Officer of Hupeh; appointed Magistrate of Lung-hsing (in modern Kiangsi province) and Pacification Officer of Kiangsi.

1178   Given the title of Lord Assistant Chief Justice.

1179   Appointed Assistant Fiscal Intendant (*Chuan-yün fu-shih*) of Hupeh, and then of Hunan; appointed Magistrate of T'an-chou and Pacification Officer of Hunan.

1180   Initiated reforms and organized, against Imperial edict, the Flying Tigers Army of Hunan; given the title of Editor of Yu-wen Palace; assigned to Kiangsi as Magistrate of Lung-hsing and Pacification Officer.

1181   Built his villa at Ribbon Lake; assumed the style-name of Chia-hsüan.

1182   Removed from office by Imperial Censor Wang Lin.

1182–   Lived in retirement at his villa in Shang-jao.
1192

1188   First volume (*chüan* "chia") of Hsin's collected lyrics printed under the supervision of Fan K'ai (the fourth and last *chüan* completed in 1203).

1192   Appointed Judicial Intendant of Fukien.

1193   Summoned for an audience with Emperor Kuang-tsung; given the title of Editor of Chi-ying Palace and appointed Magistrate of Foochow and Pacification Officer of Fukien.

1194   Removed from administrative duties in Fukien by Imperial Censor Huang Ai, made Guardian of Ch'ung-yu Temple at Mount Wu-i in Fukien; stripped of the title as Editor of Imperial Archives.

1195   Removed from the Temple guardianship by Imperial Censor Ho Tan; returned to Shang-jao.

1196   Villa destroyed by fire; moved to Ch'i-ssu, in Ch'ien-shan *hsien*.

1203   Appointed Magistrate of Shao-hsing and Pacification Officer of Che-tung district.

1204   Summoned for an audience with Emperor Ning-tsung; appointed Magistrate of Chen-chiang and given the title of Academician-in-waiting (*tai-chih*) of Pao-mo Pavilion.

1206   Declined appointment of administrative posts in Chekiang; given additional titles as Academician-in-waiting of Pao-wen Pavilion and of Lung-t'u Pavilion.

1207   Summoned to the capital for another audience with Emperor Ning-tsung; declined appointment as Transmitter of Directives in the Bureau of Military Affairs (*shu-mi ch'eng-chih*); died in Ch'ien-shan on October 3, 1207 (10th day of the 9th lunar month).

CHAPTER 1

The Making of a Chinese Poet

> Man exists as a unity-in-tension of
> four modes of being: soul, body,
> mind and spirit. . . . As body and
> mind, man is a natural creature, as
> soul and spirit, a historical person.
> —W. H. Auden, "The Virgin &
> The Dynamo," *The Dyer's
> Hand*

Poetry, the oldest and the most exalted literary profession in China, is an art that requires of its practitioners the most stringent demands in the use of language; and yet the products of a poet's pen, at least during his own lifetime, were often overshadowed by the fame associated with his personality, by his public career, or by his accomplishments in other and more "important" fields of scholarship. One is inclined to say, then, that poetry among the Chinese is engaged in by professionals (with words) who are nonprofessionals (in attitude), since their normal day-to-day energy is directed elsewhere. A Chinese poet might have been a monk or an emperor, a general or a recluse, a prime minister and statesman or a poor scholar and an unsuccessful candidate for a degree. Many of the poets, too, were equally well known by their reputation in other arts—as an essayist, a musician, or a master painter or calligrapher. The career of a Chinese poet finds analogies in the West only in the life of those few who combined literary pursuit with public service— men like Dante, Chaucer, Spenser, Milton, or Swift, or, among the moderns, most strikingly, Dag Hammarskjöld.

The life and philosophy of a Chinese poet, therefore, are always closely interwoven into the fabric of a poem, however beguilingly it might have been written on a very minor subject. Each poem is a product of the moment, born of a tension created between the properties of the language and life's hopes and aspirations—in other words, between form and content; a poet's life *is* the material of his poetry. And, as it had happened in the past, divisions and strife within the country, or foreign invasions, and confrontations with new philosophical ideas or art forms invariably served to heighten such a tension, resulting in poetry of high order. Marked by political instability, material abundance, and both intellectual and artistic ferment, the Southern Sung dynasty (1127–1279) was such a period; Hsin Ch'i-chi (Hsi Chia-hsüan, 1140–1207), to the Chinese a patriot as well as a major poet in the *tz'u* or "Lyric Meter"[1] tradition, was a product of this culture.

I *A Divided China*

Hsin Ch'i-chi was born on May 28, 1140 (the eleventh day of the fifth month of the year *keng-sheng,* being the tenth year of the reign Shao-hsing under Emperor Kao-tsung) in Li-ch'eng (modern Tsinan in Shantung province), when Northern China had been for thirteen years under the rule of the Chin (also spelled Kin) dynasty. The dynasty was founded by the Jurchëd (also spelled Jurchen, or Nü-chen, and sometimes also called the Tartars), a Tungustic people from the northern part of Manchuria, who had, while posing as allies of the Northern Sung, helped to defeat her erstwhile enemy, the Khitans (*Ch'i-tan*), a seminomadic Mongol tribe from southern Manchuria who had founded the Liao dynasty (947–1125) to the north of the Sung Empire. After the conquest of Liao, the Jurchëd marched into Pien-ching (modern K'ai-feng in Honan province), the capital of the Northern Sung, and captured the last emperor Ch'in-tsung and his father, Emperor Hui-tsung, better known to posterity as a poet and painter of flowers and birds. A son of Emperor Hui-tsung, known as Emperor Kao-tsung (*r.* 1127–62), established his court in Lin-an (modern Hangchow in Chekiang province) and founded what was to be known later as the Southern Sung dynasty.

The unoccupied China in the South, though flourishing in commerce and foreign trade, remembered the shame of the capture of the last two emperors, the repeated forays of the Chin army into the South, the humiliating annual tributes in silver and silk, the degrading terms of vassalage imposed by the rulers of the North, and the failure of their own sporadic but unsuccessful attempts at the recovery of the "Central Plains." A year after the poet's birth, the heroic general Yüeh Fei (1103–41) was secretly put to death while imprisoned, and the appeasement policy advocated by Prime Minister Ch'in Kuei (?–1155) was maintained. In the same year, the first of a series of peace treaties was concluded between the Southern Sung and the Chin empires.

In 1149, an ambitious sinicized Jurchëd ruler, Prince Hai-ling (whose cruelty and licentiousness became the favorite subject of many a storyteller in Hangchow in later years[2]), murdered his way to the Chin throne and moved his capital four years later from Yenching (modern Peking) to K'ai-feng. He is also said to have become so enamored of the beauty of Hangchow that he decided, in 1161, to wage a major campaign for its capture. The attack was successfully repulsed, Prince Hai-ling was murdered by his own general, and the Chin army withdrew. In 1163, the new Sung emperor Hsiao-tsung (r. 1163–89), under the advice of Prime Minister Chang Chün (?–1164), started a counteroffensive which, however, ended in defeat at the Battle of Fu-li (in modern Anhwei province) and in a new peace treaty in 1165. Both Emperor Hsiao-tsung and his successor Kuang-tsung (r. 1190–94) were feeble rulers, and the ineptitude of the Sung court resulted in the schemings of the Empress Li and the rise of the unsavory politician Han T'o-chou (?–1207), who recommended the adoption of a war policy during the reign of Ningtsung (1195–1224). The patriotic sentiments of Hsin Ch'i-chi were adroitly exploited by Han, who assumed the prime ministership in 1195; but the disastrous war (1204–7) he conducted ended again in defeat. The year of Hsin's death, 1207, also saw the execution of Han T'o-chou, whose head was proffered to the Chin ruler in the North as one of the conditions for a new peace treaty.

II *An Obscure Boyhood*

Not much is known of Hsin Ch'i-chi's life before 1162 when the poet moved South. According to his own account, he was brought up by a stern and patriotic grandfather, Hsin Tsan, magistrate of Po-chou (in the northern part of modern Anhwei province), who was unable, because of his large family, to follow the government into exile [PP 3]. According to an account of a near-contemporary of the poet, Yüan Hao-wen (1190–1257), he studied under a famous scholar of Po-chou by the name of Liu Chan (Liu Yen-lao; *fl.* 1153, who won the *chin-shih* degree in 1151 and became Compiler in the Archives of History in 1161).[3] Also, according to this account, corroborated by the official biography of the poet in the *Sung shih*

[History of the Sung Dynasty], he had as his classmate a boy six years his senior, Tang Huai-ying (1134–1211), who later became a literary luminary of the Chin court and held many high posts, including the Directorship of Education (*kuo-tzu chi-chiu*).

Before Hsin made up his mind to go South, a year after his grandfather's death, the poet and his classmate consulted the *Book of Changes* (*I ching*), an ancient classic of divination, to help them arrive at a decision. Probably by using yarrowstalks, Tang obtained the hexagram "k'an" (number 29☵), the sign of the "abysmal," or water; while our poet drew as his answer the hexagram "li" (number 30☲), the sign of the "clinging," or fire. The first hexagram is interpreted as foretelling of "ensnarement"; it cautions one "to proceed along the sign of the least resistance" but promises "success in teaching" to a "man of sincerity."[4] Tang decided to remain in the North. The hexagram "li," on the other hand, is said by the Commentary of the *I ching* to embody "the forces of light and . . . of spiritual life," "to stand in the south," and to represent "the summer sun, which illumines all earthly things."[5] While it predicts "confusion of daily business," it also promises "Tears in floods, sighing and lamenting./ Good fortune."[6] Obeying the oracular message that "That which is bright rises twice,"[7] the poet left his native city for the court in Hangchow.

III *Youthful Exploits*

The hexagram obtained by Hsin at this turning point in his life also says that when "Nine is at the top,"

> The king uses him to march forth and chastise,
> Then it is best to kill the leaders
> And take captive the followers. No blame.[8]

As if to demonstrate the magic of the *I ching* in foretelling the future, according to what Carl Jung calls the "principle of synchronicity" as opposed to the concept of causality,[9] the events immediately following the poet's journey South worked out in precisely the pattern predicted. In the winter of 1161–62, there had been numerous anti-Jurchëd uprisings in his native province of Shantung; among the leaders of these peasant rebellions was a man named Ken Ching, also of Tsinan, who commanded a force of considerable size and gave himself the title of the "Commandant of Heavenly Peace."

Hsin decided to join him and persuaded others to do the same, including a monk named I-tuan, "who loved to talk about strategy." The latter turned out to be a renegade and one night fled from the camp with the seal of the commandant. Greatly angered by the theft, Ken threatened to kill the poet for having recommended the monk to him; and Hsin unhesitatingly replied, "Give me three days, and if I do not capture the monk I will answer with my own life." Hsin raided the enemy camp and found his former friend, who pleaded with him: "I recognize you from your physiognomy to be the incarnation of a blue rhinoceros. Please spare me."[10] (The poet is described by a contemporary as a man "of massive shoulders and flashing eyes."[11] Hsin brought back the head of the renegade monk to redeem his promise.

In January, 1162, Hsin led a mission, as Ken Ching's secretary, to the refined court of Emperor Kao-tsung. The rebel delegation was granted an audience in Chien-k'ang (modern Nanking), and both Ken and Hsin were rewarded with titles and insignia of office. One day when the poet was absent from the camp on a mission, Ken was murdered by one of his followers, Chang An-kuo, who had surrendered to the Jurchëd side. Upon his return and discovery of this betrayal, Hsin led a small posse, said to be of some fifty men,[12] to raid the enemy camp. He found Chang reveling among the Chin generals, tied him to a horse, dragged him away, and had him executed at the market place. These acts of heroism earned for our poet his first assignment, as Signatory Official (*ch'ien-p'an*) on the prefectural staff of Chiang-yin (modern Chen-chiang in northern Kiangsu province), where he served for two years (1162–64).

IV *The Kingdom's Task:*
His "Ten Discourses" and "Nine Treatises"

Not long after the poet had moved South, though no exact date can be ascertained, Hsin married the daughter of Fan Pang-yen (1099–1172), who, like Hsin, was from the North and who, as magistrate of Ts'ai-chou on the border region, had surrendered his city to the court of the Southern Sung in 1161. The records are not clear as to the whereabouts of the poet between 1164 and 1168, when he was appointed to the staff of Magistrate Shih Chih-tao of Nanking, again as Signatory Official.

Probably in 1168 or two or three years earlier,[13] the poet presented to the throne a series of ten essays under the collective title of "The Humble Offering of Ten Discourses" (*Mei-ch'in shih-lun*). The titles, which I have either translated or paraphrased (and occasionally included brief summaries of the content), are as follows:

1. (*Shen-shih*) On the Importance of Assessing the Strength and the Weaknesses [of the Enemy]; that territorial size, wealth and the size of the army refer to physical things and must be distinguished from "forces" (*shih*) that should be reckoned with.

2. (*Ch'a-ch'ing*) On the Importance of Spying; that when to talk peace and when to fight should be determined by our knowledge of the enemy situation: whether they genuinely desire peace or they are too weak to wage war.

3. (*Kuan-ch'ou*) How to Take Advantage of the Discontent of the People under Enemy Rule.

4. (*Tzu-chih*) Self-rule; that history does not necessarily repeat the lesson that the South is too weak to reconquer the "Central Plains."

5. (*Shou-Huai*) The Importance of Defending the Huai River region.

6. (*Tun-t'ien*) How to Modify the Policy of Making Landtillers out of Soldiers; that the failures of this policy in the past have been due to the soldiers' not being "expert" enough; that this shortcoming can be corrected by accepting deserters who know how to farm and who are already familiar with the area.

7. (*Chih-yung*) How to Build up the Morale of the Army; that the emperor must reward soldiers and generals alike; that the tasks of the soldiers must be lightened and both rewards and condolences for those lost in battle should reach the troop fast.

8. (*Fang-wei*) How to Prevent People from Becoming Enemy Spies and How to Attract More Deserters from the Other Side.

9. (*Chiu-jen*) The Importance of Placing Confidence upon Ministers; that an able general should not have been removed after just one defeat.

10. (*Hsiang-chang*) A Detailed Discussion on Warfare; that attack is preferable to defense ("When two nations face each other, one built on deceit and the other living in constant fear, war is inevitable"); that it is important in fighting to seize geographical advantages ("Attack the body of the snake rather than its head or tail"); that a reconquest of the Central Plains presupposes taking Hopei and the road to Hopei lies through Shantung; that the people

of Shantung are known for their bravery and for their recalcitrance in times of trouble [PP3–23].

The opinions expressed in these "discourses" reflect, no doubt, Hsin's observation of the South during the last few years as well as his memories of the North. Even as late as 1168, only three years after the peace treaty, they must have provided some uncomfortable reading. Significantly, the longest of the ten compositions, "A Detailed Discussion on Warfare," was placed last. It must have been an equally difficult job for the poet to argue against a cyclical interpretation of history, as he attempted in Number 4 (the second longest piece), where he took great pains to point out the fallacy of a parallel with the history of other periods of division in China: the Three Kingdoms (220–80) and the Six Dynasties (222–589) periods. Particularly the Six Dynasties (those that had their capital in Nanking)—consisting of Wu of the Three Kingdoms, Eastern Chin (317–420), Liu Sung (420–79), Southern Ch'i (479–502), Liang (502–57), and Ch'en (557–89)—provide numerous allusions in his poetry.

In 1169, when Yü Yün-wen (1110–74), a former prime minister who, in 1161, had defeated the Jurchëd at the Battle of the Colorful Stone Jetty (Ts'ai-shih chi) on the Yangtze, was reappointed to the same post, the time seemed to the poet more propitious for advocating military actions against the Chin Empire. Accordingly, he wrote for the new prime minister a series of proposals under the title of "Nine Treatises" (*Chiu-i*). Carrying no subtitles, the nine sections deal with more specific policies to prepare for a resumption of war. Except for two sections (Nos. 6 and 9) which repeat assertions made earlier—namely, that the South must retake Shantung and that one must not subscribe to the theory of a permanent division between the North and the South—the rest of the treatise is given to outlining concrete measures of reform. To shatter the opposition, the poet argued at the outset that "My idea is not to risk everything in a single throw [of dice]; war indeed is a dangerous affair, but to banish or taboo all wars requires the knowledge of how to fight them" [PP 24]. Other opinions expressed reveal, equally clearly, the mind of a military strategist; such as "Success in battle is based on deceit, and deceit requires that one must appear haughty to the enemy and try to tire them and create dissension among their rank and file" [PP 28], or "When the enemy presses for a quick result, we adopt defensive measures" [PP 28], or "A victorious army wins before going into battle; a defeated army seeks battle before having any plans" [PP 28]. Among the plans he outlined, he proposed the use of intelligence ("In my travels in the North [before 1162] I have seen the enemy use alum shale (*fan-[shih]*)) with which to steep the paper on which the written message remains invisible until submerged in water" [PP 28]; three years of wartime economy in order to enrich the treasury before terminating the tributes; the need to discourage talks about moving the capital to Nanking (a step he had advocated earlier), but count on a surprise move when everything is ready; and the urgent task of stopping all private feuds between the Northerners and the Southerners in court [PP 31–34]. These bold and far-reaching measures, however, failed to win the court's adoption; they succeeded only in winning for the poet, in 1170, another audience with the emperor and appointment to the Ministry of Agriculture and two years later the post of a magistrate of Ch'u-chou (in modern Anhwei).

V *Ten Years of Administrative Work*

Situated between two major rivers, the city of Ch'u-chou had some strategic importance, but through the ravage of war and four years of flood it had become a poverty-stricken area, with only fewer than half of the former population being resettled. Upon assuming office, Hsin requested the throne for a remission of taxes, made loans available to the inhabitants for the repair of their houses, and reduced taxes on transient businessmen by 30 percent in order to attract a larger volume of commerce. Aided by these measures and a good wheat harvest the following year, the city prospered; and in 1172 the poet decreed the building, for public use, of a pavilion which he named Pavilion of Peace and Order (Tien-chen lou). Upon its completion, he invited his friend and Professor of Chen-chou Academy, Chou Fu (1135–77), to come for a visit. The latter was so moved by the sight that he wrote both a "descriptive record" (*chi*)[14] and a rhyme-prose composition (*fu*)[15] about the building. Another man of letters, Ts'ui Tun-li (*fl.* 1178), commissioned by a friend of Hsin's, also wrote a "descriptive record"[16] of this pavilion, the first of many building projects that the poet undertook all during his life.

In 1173, Hsin received an "exemplary recommendation" (*chi-pien t'ui-shang*)[17] for his administration of Ch'u-chou; a year later, enjoying the confidence of a new prime minister, Yeh Heng (1122–83), he was appointed to the Ministry of Grains. In 1175, he addressed to the throne a memorial on the importance of not devaluating the paper currency (*hui-tzu*);[18] in the summer of the same year he was sent to Hunan to suppress an insurrection of tea farmers led by a notorious tea merchant, Lai Wen-cheng. Following the successful conclusion of this campaign and the execution of Lai by a ruse, the poet won appointment as Judicial Intendant (*t'i-tien hsing-yü*) of Kiangsi and the honorary title of the Compilorship of Imperial Archives (*pi-ko hsiu-chuan*). Between 1174 and 1178, Hsin served at various posts in Kiangsi and Hupeh, either as Pacification Officer (*an-wu-shih*) or as magistrate. During terms of office, he was not afraid to censure either magistrates or army officers. In 1178, he achieved the highest rank of his official career when he was made Lord Assistant Chief Justice (*ta-li shao-ch'ing*), a title of the "full" sixth rank.[19]

In 1179, Hsin was sent to Hunan as Pacification Officer and magistrate of T'an-chou, where for many years peasant uprisings had been especially rife. Hsin immediately addressed a memorial on the need to remove the cause of the trouble by bettering the life of the peasants.[20] At the same time, he launched many projects: he issued government rice to pay for the construction of dikes, reduced the size of "village societies" from several hundred families to no larger than fifty, confiscated weapons, established schools, and, against local opposition, made the manufacture of wine a government monopoly. But the most controversial act of his career was the organization, in 1180, of the Flying Tigers Army (*Fei-hu chün*) of Hunan.

Recognizing the need for a militia of well-trained soldiers to be used purely for local defense and under local command, Hsin started on this project without waiting for the court's approval. He selected a campsite, built barracks, advertised for a volunteer army of two thousand foot soldiers and five hundred cavalry soldiers, and ordered horses to be purchased from Kwangsi.[21] Upon being informed of these activities, the court looked upon the costliness and the ambitiousness of the project with alarm and dispatched "gold-letter tablets from the throne" (*yü-ch'ien chin tzu-p'ai*) in an effort to stop the construction. The barracks were still a month away from completion when the tablets reached him, but Hsin chose to hide the court's order and to proceed with his plan. A long rainy season also happened to delay the making of roof-tiles; discovering that the need was for twenty thousand pieces of tiles, Hsin ordered each family to contribute twenty tiles taken from their own houses.[22] The project was completed on schedule, and he presented to the emperor a map of the Flying Tiger Army camp as his reply to the "gold-letter tablets."

Despite much adverse criticism directed at the lavish expenditure for this army, the letters and memorials from several of Hsin's contemporaries, including the Neo-Confucianist philosopher Chu Hsi (1130–1200), praised the effectiveness of the project in maintaining peace and order in the region for many years beyond Hsin's term of office.[23] For example, in Chu Hsi's memorial to the throne, he pointed out that such later troubles as the unruliness of the soldiers was due not to Hsin's original design but to a shift of command when the army was ordered to be attached to the district capital of Hsiang-yang.[24] This most celebrated enterprise in the poet's middle career earned him the censure of the court, but received the approbation of the discerning few.

In 1181, Hsin was appointed the Pacification Officer of Kiangsi, which was then suffering from starvation. He succeeded in controlling the situation by issuing an order in eight words which, translated into English, read: "He who refuses to sell rice will be conscripted; he who forces the purchase of rice upon others will be executed."[25] His forthrightness and courage in this and other projects won him many enemies. In the winter of this year, Imperial Censor Wang Lin lodged against the poet an accusation with the use of two clichés; namely, that Hsin "used money like dirt and sand" and "took people's lives as if plucking out grass and weeds."[26] This charge of extravagance and callousness finally caused Hsin to be removed from his last poet as district Fiscal Intendant in Chekiang (Liang-Che *lu*).

Hsin lived through several demotions and two major censures. The second censure came in 1194, at the end of his second and shorter stint as an official (1192–94), when he was relieved of the post of Fiscal Intendant (*chuan-yün shih*) of Fukien. According to the historical record, Hsin harbored the belief that Fukien, being a coastal area, was a breeding ground of "robbers and insurrectionists" and that the people there were hard to govern. Accordingly, in Foochow, in order to prepare for bad years of harvest, he built a Reserve Treasury (*Pei-an k'u*) to enable the government to purchase rice in good years and thus to achieve self-sufficiency in grain. This Reserve Treasury is said to have accumulated at one time 500,000 strings of cash (*min*);

for this Hsin was accused of "cruelty and greed" and of having emptied the entire city of its wealth.[27]

The career of a Confucian official during the Sung dynasty was marked by an unusual degree of turbulence. The threat of a renewed invasion from the North was not as real as the fear of party cliques. This fear was expressed by Emperor Hsiao-tsung in a decree, in 1190, that "while the rightness or wrongness of Court policy can certainly be debated, pure argument (*ch'ing-i*) must not be encouraged, for it will invariably lead to the formation of parties which brought an end to the Eastern Han dynasty."[28] Hence, recommendations from powerful ministers were chiefly relied upon as a guarantee of one's loyalty and talent; but the political fortunes of even the great rose and fell rather swiftly. Probably similar to the "exile mentality" which prevailed during the Six Dynasties period, such a condition, aggravated by a huge bureaucracy, easily encouraged flattery in court and led to an increase in the power of eunuchs, as happened during the reigns of Emperors Kuang-tsung and Ning-tsung. It is not surprising, therefore, that Hsin not only looked with admiration upon those men of talent and character of the earlier era, but also, above everything else, prized in himself as well as in his friends, a quality of moral rectitude known in Chinese as *ch'i-chieh,* which generally means "an unswerving loyalty to principles and an unblemished integrity of character." That he became known in China as a "patriotic poet" par excellence is no accident, but his loyalty was not to the emperor alone. His poetry is not that of a poet laureate, but the voice of a misunderstood and tortured intellectual.

VI   *Twenty Years of Contemplative Life*

It is not unusual for those brought up on the teachings of Confucius to remember the Master's command that "it is a thing of shame to receive remuneration from the state when those in power have forsaken the Way."[29] Therefore, to withdraw from the frenzy of politics to a life free from burdens in the country is not an uncommon outcome for Chinese scholar-officials. Hsin Ch'i-chi, however, is distinguished from many others by the wholehearted and deliberate way in which he lived the life of a recluse. The years after 1182 became the most productive period of his poetical career; no more than one-tenth of his extant lyrics, which number over six hundred, can be dated to have been written before his "retirement."

For his retreat from the political arena, Hsin chose to settle in the county of Shang-jao ("Upper Abundance," so called because of its fertile land; there is also a county of the same name situated in the lower bend of the river, which is called Hsia-jao),[30] in Hsin-chou *hsien* (in modern Kiangsi near the border with Fukien). Hsin-chou was then a rather large metropolitan center about two hundred miles southeast of the capital, Hangchow. To the north of the city is a scenic mountain called Lin-shan (Spirit Mountain); there he bought land and built a rather large estate facing a lake named Tai-hu, or Ribbon (also translated as Sash) Lake, which must have derived its name from its being always smooth and calm. To one of the buildings in the compound, he gave the name of "Chia-hsüan" ("Farming Pavilion"), after which he adopted the style-name (*hao*) of "Chia-hsüan chü-shih" ("Master of the Farming Pavilion"). (The term *Chü-shih* originally meant "a Buddhist layman.")

After a fire destroyed the villa in 1196, the poet moved to nearby Ch'ien-shan (Lead Mountain) *hsien,* to a place called Ch'i-ssu. Except for the three years (1192–95) when he served at official posts in Fukien and the two years (1203–5) when he was recalled to Chekiang, Hsin enjoyed nearly two decades (1182–1207) of a life of leisure among the mountains and the lakes which he loved. A description of his villa and its surroundings may be found in the "Descriptive Record of the Farming Pavilion" (*Chia-hsüan chi*), written at his request by one of his friends, Hung Mai (1123–1202), a noted diarist and versatile scholar:

The land is adjacent to the city on three sides, but faces a clear lake in front, which stretches like a piece of precious ribbon or sash [*pao-tai*], and which is over twelve or thirteen hundred feet long and about eight hundred thirty feet wide. . . . Few people knew the beauty of this spot . . . until Hsin Yu-an [the poet's courtesy-name] of Tsinan came. Here he built a house of a hundred pillars [or units, *ying*], which occupies only forty per cent of the land area. He turned the land to the left of the house into rice-fields, where he expects to farm after being relieved of official duties. The house which commands a view from a height is the so-called "Farming Pavilion" . . . as if he really wished to make his living with a hoe . . . .[31]

His villa soon became so famous that his friend Ch'en Liang (Ch'en T'ung-fu, 1143–94) mentioned in a letter to him that their philosopher-friend Chu Hsi had once "sneaked" into the house while to view the scenery of the Wu-i Mountains in northern Fukien. Hsin described this trip in a series of ten poems, written in the traditional quatrain (*chüeh-chü*) style, in which he referred to his friend as "a teacher of kings." On the other hand, in a letter to the poet, Chu commended Hsin for his "manifest, rare talent" and his ever-present desire to become "the legs and arms" of the emperor.[39] Chu died in 1200, five years after Han T'o-chou, the enemy of many intellectuals at the time, had become the prime minister. Chu's philosophy had been banned by the government since 1195 as "false learning" (*wei-hsüeh*), and at his funeral the court considered the need to restrict the size of the funeral procession lest such an occasion lead to "erroneous criticism of government policy."[40] According to the official biography of our poet in the *Sung shih,* many of Chu's pupils and friends did not dare attend the funeral. Yet, despite the official policy Hsin publicly eulogized his philosopher-friend and wrote, "th which is immortal [in Chu] will last ten thousand generations."[41]

S. Chu Hsi's dislike of Taoism is well known,[42] the friendship bet Chu and Hsin more than testifies to mutual respect; it indi-ca think, the breadth of vision of two of the most eclectic minds of thern Sung dynasty. Chu devoted his life to the study of the relationship to the universe and succeeded in systematiz-ian thought by building upon the tenets of thinkers of g dynasty; namely, Chou Tun-i (1017–73), Chang 77) and the two Ch'eng brothers, Ch'eng Hao (1032– ng I (1033–1107). Hsin's accomplishment as a lyricist parable, at least in character and scope, in the world of of his friend in philosophy. Hsin took the form of the hich had already become popular with poets of the uch as Ou-yang Hsiu (1007–1072), Chou Pang-yen Shih (Su Tung-p'o, 1036–1101), Li Ch'ing-chao many others, and succeeded in extending its range es and enriching its conventions. He revitalized it with his own personality, his gift of language, t as the Neo-Confucianists met the challenge of reting the doctrines of Confucius and Mencius from the ancient classics, Hsin broke new infusing it with ancient Chinese poetic tradi-new mode.

he was absent and came away describing it as "something never seen or heard of by men."[32]

Another document, "An Address to the Spirits upon Putting up the Beam of My New House" (*Shang-liang wen*), expresses the poet's intentions and desires in more descriptive and personal terms. In this short essay, which includes six verse stanzas near the end, he wrote:

To spend a huge sum of money for a house and a larger sum for the neighborhood: no happiness in life is treasured more than to live in peace. It takes a year to harvest and ten years to grow a tree: a superior man [*chün-tzu*] always harbors the intention to retire. I have long tired of moving from one place to another, and now I seek a propitious place for my home. I, the Master of the Farming Pavilion, grew up in the Northwest, became an official in the Southwest, having served both in court and twice on military posts, and three times enjoyed the privilege of being summoned by the Emperor. Now that my hands, used to wind and frost, are about to show wrinkles like the veins on the back of a tortoise, and my hair, as a result of my chasing after profit and fame, is about to turn white like that of a crane—I seek a little place of my own. Though situated in the country, it is uniquely free of the clamour and the dust of horses and carriages. A house on the green mountain, thousands of ancient trees, the white water at fields' edge, and acres of lotus! There will be paths criss-crossing the fields, fishermen and woodcutters to rejoice with, and children and women to laugh together! To dream about the time of my youth spent in the saddle, and to be immersed in the poetry and the classics of the ancients! Although it could be said that riches and honor have forsaken me, I feel myself that the woods and the streams have extended me an invitation. I look forward to the pleasure of roaming beyond things, but I also love my hut.[33] I say to those who struggle and swim with the current: "You go your way, and I go mine."[34] I raise the tall pillar, and I rejoice in the beam's being put in its place.

Raise the beam to the east:
Let me sit and watch the morning sun burst into a tall flame.
Even if I am free, like a guest, to roam the rivers and sea,
I should worry about the nation's welfare and wish for a bountiful harvest.

Raise the beam to the west:
For ten thousand *li,* I have lost my way among rivers and lakes.
A native of the Northwest,[35] and of a general's true blood;
Still it may be a good idea to sell one's sword to purchase a hoe and a
    plow.

Raise the beam to the south:
I open my window to say farewell to the sun sinking beyond small hills.
Around the forest, the magpies are secure on their branches;
Pillowed in the warm breeze, I am sound asleep.

Raise the beam to the north:
The road from the capital is buried in dust, all messages cut off.
All my life, I am fit only to remain in Changsha;[36]
I wish to strike the chieftain, but lack the strength because of age.

Raise the beam upward:
But let me not aspire to the Heavenly Gate guarded by tigers and
    leopards;[37]
I further need the Heavenly Maiden[38] to scatter the heavenly flowers
So that I can visit often with Vimalakirti in his small cell.

Lower the beam downward:
With wine and chicken, what is the time to visit the neighbors' house?
Only now the Master [*chü-shih*] has his new nest:
He wishes to stop at the window [*hsüan*] to see much farming [*chia*]
    done. [PP 39–40]

In this autobiographical account, the poet views his past career with some nostalgia but without bitterness. His mind dwells on the fate of China's banished poets, and he tempers Confucian aspiration with a philosophical attitude. Directing his thoughts upward, he makes references to the life of a Buddhist layman and contemporary of Buddha—known as Vimalakirti in Sanskrit or as Wei-mo-chieh in Chinese (from whose name the T'ang poet Wang Wei (699–759) took the last two characters as his style-name and also the word *wei* as his personal name)—and to the pleasure of "roaming beyond things" (*wu-wei hsiao-yao*), or nonattachment, terms derived from the writings of the Taoist philosopher Chuang Tzu, which became Hsin's favorite book during his retirement. Observing the more earthly pleasures of life, he speaks of hills and streams and of woodcutters and other country people, which will be among the chief sources of imagery in many of his lyrics.

VII   *The Poet's Circle of Friends*

Hsin's villa on Ribbon Lake, or his second home in Ch'ien-shan, located near a scenic spring called P'iao-ch'üan (Gourd Spring), provides the poet with the setting for receiving occasional visitors from among his many friends and younger contemporaries. strong personality and his colorful career no doubt contribute his pre-eminence. It is rather curious that, despite the poet's preference for the Taoist philosophy, Hsin numbered among his circle of friends nearly all the important thinkers of his tim pounders of what came to be known in the West as Neo-Cor ism or *li-hsüeh* in Chinese, the "School of Principle" (sc translated as Reason). Among these men were Chang Shih Nan-hsüan, 1133–80) and Lü Tsu-ch'ien (Lü Po-kung, or lai, 1137–81), both of whom died shortly before the poet's Shang-jao. Among the others of this group whose friendsh became more intimate, after 1182, were: Chu Hsi, th thesizer of Confucian thought and the founder of th wing of Neo-Confucianism; Lu Chiu-yüan (Lu Hsian 92), Chu's archrival and founder of the idealistic w doctrine, known as the School of the Mind (*hsin-hs* Liang, more a man of action than a philosopher, f Yung-k'ang (Chekiang) branch of Neo-Confuc patriot, and perhaps Hsin's closest friend. (Af sented to the throne, in 1178, five essays on "I Nation" (*Chung-hsing wu-lun*) and later suffere on false charges, he passed the "Presented examination in 1193, a year before his death.)

Among Hsin's younger contemporaries t 1182), who began in 1188 to supervise t lected lyrics, "in order to stop all spurio (he wrote in a preface for the first vol year); Huang Kan (1152–1221), one and Liu Kuo (1154–1206), a lyric tor. Then there were others: historia like Li T'ao (1115–84), Hung whose collected works Hsin su Chou's death; high-ranking of like Fan Ch'eng-ta (1126–9 whom were among the fin poetry.

In 1188, Ch'en Liang ten days; they toured be joined by Chu H
In 1193, Hsin visit

CHAPTER 2

The Evolution of the Lyric Meter

> The literary man is a specialist in association ('wit'), dissociation ('judgment'), recombination (making a new whole out of elements separately experienced). He uses words as his medium.
> —René Wellek and Austin Warren, *Theory of Literature*

Certain aspects of a culture which most deeply touch the people's daily life are invariably reflected in the creation of a particularized vocabulary by which they refer to these aspects. As anthropologists have pointed out, the language of the Eskimo has no single word for "snow" but abounds in separate words to describe the different kinds of snow.[1] Further illustrations are the nomenclatures of Japanese tea ceremony or of American jazz, where the distinctions between one term and another are known only to the initiated. Similarly, Westerners who can tell the difference between a Celadon and a *sang-de-boeuf* vase may not be aware of the numerous distinctions of color of Chinese porcelain, such as "sweet white" (*tien-pai*), "sacrificial red" (*chi-hung*), or "misty blue-green" (*ying-ch'ing*), or any of the names of the twenty-two major kilns (*yao*) in Sung China alone,[2] by which geographical names ("Chün yao," "Chien yao," etc.) the porcelain wares are known among the Chinese.

In the literati-dominated society of China, therefore, it should come as no surprise that the word *shih* ("poetry") is used by the Chinese either to refer to the ancient anthology known as the *Shih ching* (*Book of Poetry*) or in the broadest way to designate the class of rhymed compositions in general in contradistinction to prose (*wen*). The "poems" they write are always referred to by the names of the specific subgenre to which the poem belongs; such as "ancient poetry" (*ku-shih*), "regulated verse" (*lü-shih*), "broken-off lines" or quatrains (*chüeh-chü*), and *tz'u*. This abundance of literary terms is comparable to the debt owed by the English language to the culture of the ancient Greeks who have bequeathed us such common words as "comedy," "tragedy," "elegy," "ode," "epithalamium," and the word "lyric" itself.

I   The Word "Tz'u" Defined

In its broadest sense, the word *tz'u* means "no more than 'words (for singing),' "[3] as James J. Y. Liu points out in *The Art of Chinese Poetry*. This interpretation is based upon the commentaries made by a Ch'ing scholar Tuan Yü-ts'ai (1735–1815) upon the earliest Chinese dictionary, compiled around 100 A.D., where this word is defined as "the exterior [*wai*] expression [*yen*] of what is felt inside [*i-nei*]"[4] and is glossed by him as meaning "the perfect matching (*ho*) of sound and shape [i.e., words]." But there exists in the Chinese language another character with the same pronunciation, which denotatively also means "words,"[5] but frequently connotes "the embellishment of speech" or "the description of things and situations," two definitions which are also recorded by Tuan in the same gloss mentioned earlier. Although Tuan offers the theory that the two homophones are altogether of different origin and meaning, the use of these two words as synonyms by ancient writers (including China's first historian, Ssu-ma Ch'ien of the first century B.C.)[6] is quite common. It is not inconceivable, therefore, that the concept of "embellishment" must have somehow entered into the meaning of the first *tz'u,* as that word became current much later as the name of a subgenre of Chinese poetry.

Specifically, *tz'u* refers to one kind of Chinese verse which evolved around the middle of the T'ang dynasty, found ready acceptance by the poets of the tenth century, and reached the zenith of its development during the Northern Sung (960–1126) and the Southern Sung (1127–1279) dynasties. But what served as its prototype, like the problem of an *Ur-Hamlet,* still puzzles scholars. Based on scanty and conflicting earlier accounts, no more than a tentative identification is possible. It is believed by some to have been evolved from poems composed in the style of folk songs and known in Chinese as the Music Bureau (*yüeh-fu*) poetry; others ascribe its origin to the five- or seven-word quatrains perfected by T'ang poets. Still others have found isolated examples of even earlier verse and consider them the spiritual ancestors of the *tz'u*.

II *Tz'u and Music*

What is certain, however, is that "*tz'u*-poetry" (if the redundancy can be allowed) emerged at a time when innovations were being made in the style of chanting poems and in singing. Such a change occurred in the middle of the eighth century as the result of new knowledge of foreign music and musical instruments brought back from central Asia and elsewhere to the T'ang empire. Refrains (*ho-sheng*) and sometimes meaningless, extra syllables called "floating sound" (*fan-sheng*), or interpolations,"[7] were often added to poems written in the quatrain style in order to make them more "singable," to adapt them to new melodies. Then, texts of new songs were composed, or said to be "filled in" (*t'ien*), to the requirements of a particular musical air, called *tiao* (generally translated as "tune-patterns" or "melody-types"[8])—somewhat in the manner the words of the familiar Christmas song "What Child Is This?" can be said to have been written "to the tune of" the Elizabethan air "Greensleeves."

This practice was already popular with the poets of the late T'ang, such as Wen T'ing-yün (?812–?870), who might have written many of his extant lyrics for the royal "music institute" called *chiao-fang*; but it did not become widespread until the tenth century, when it came under the aegis of the royal patronage in at least two kingdoms —Shu (modern Szechwan) and the Southern T'ang (937–75), whose last emperor, Li Yü (937–78), was a recognized master of this genre. The greatest musical inspiration for this type of poetry, however, was provided only with the establishment of the Northern Sung dynasty, with its capital in K'ai-feng, a city known for its splendor and gaiety.[9] Poets like Liu Yung (*d. ca.* 1050) began to compose new songs for the singsong girls in the gay quarters of the city; and the poet Chou Pang-yen was able to write his own melodies for his verse. At the same time, a wide variety of institutions in charge of music were created by imperial decree—most notably the Great Splendor Music Bureau (*Ta-sheng yüeh-fu*) with Chou Pang-yen as its supervisor. Consisting of six departments, this institution enjoyed almost two decades of existence from 1105 and recruited composers and writers from both the degree holders of previous reigns and from ordinary people who only knew music.[10]

Gradually, however, musical scores were considered by many poets (even before the end of the Northern Sung dynasty) as of only secondary importance when scholar-officials like Ou-yang Hsiu and Su Shih began to write this style of poetry purely for personal enjoyment. With the fall of the capital to the invaders in 1126, the loss of musical source material must have hastened the demise of the vogue of writing "for" the existing tunes. This situation is reflected in an entry in the diary of Chou Mi (1232–1308), himself a lyric poet, who recorded having seen a set of "Compilation of (Musical) Scores" (*Hun-ch'eng chi*), said to consist of "over a hundred large volumes." Significantly, he added, "of all the ancient and modern songs and lyrics [*tz'u*] preserved, half of them had only musical scores but no song-texts." [11] This collection, also known as the "Great Compendium of *Yüeh-fu* (Tunes)" (*Yüeh-fu ta-ts'un*), survived until the seventeenth century; but with its loss our knowledge of even the earlier lyrics as musical form has become still more fragmentary. A recent study of Sung musical sources has discovered from all available materials only 87 pieces of Sung music (including a majority written for ancient songs);[12] whereas, the extant *tz'u* prosody identifiable by "tune-pattern" numbers over 800, with a total of 2,306 variants according to one register of *tz'u* prosody.[13] During the process of proliferation of "tune-titles" (*tiao-ming*), lyric poetry acquired its independent form and became a separate genre, although still called "song-texts" because of its origin.

III   *Tz'u as Literary Genre*

Therefore, to translate the word *tz'u* by a single word or term in English may pose some difficulty. The term "song-poem," [14] proposed by J. R. Hightower, explains its historical origin but does not describe accurately the bulk of poems written in these meters if the specific meaning of the word "song" is insisted upon. "Poems in irregular metres," [15] proposed by Cyril Birch, succeeds in characterizing the broadest aspect of the *tz'u;* namely, it is a poem made up of lines of irregular length, as its alternative name *ch'ang-tuan-chü* (lit., "long and short verse") also implies. But the word "irregular" should not be understood in the sense of "free," inasmuch as each "tune pattern" has its own prescribed rhyme scheme and other rules including even the tonal quality of individual words in a given line. Among Chinese poetic genres, the rigidity governing *tz'u* is unrivaled. The term "Lyric Meter," [16] used by James J. Y. Liu, is most satisfactory, I think, in describing both the content, which is essentially lyrical, and the form. For the sake of convenience, nonetheless, I will not stress the use of the word "meter"; rather, I will simply adopt the term "lyric" or "lyric poetry" to refer to this specific genre—without implying, of course, that lyric poetry, in its broad sense, is found exclusively in poems written in these meters.

As a matter of fact, the contrary is closer to the truth: despite its long history and its Protean nature, Chinese poetry should be thought of as representing a single, unbroken line of development. From the two earliest anthologies of verse [the *Book of Poetry (Shih ching)*,[17] a compilation of the fifth century B.C., and the *Songs of Ch'u (Ch'u Tz'u)*,[18] two centuries later] down to the *san-ch'ü*, or "scattered (nondramatic) lyrics," contemporaneous with the development of the "dramatic lyrics" (called *ch'ü*) employed in Yüan (1279–1368) drama—the lyric character of Chinese poetry has been its most notable and most admired attribute. Through the intervening centuries, as styles changed, new modes of poetry were created and new names given. What was entitled as "ancient poetry" (*ku-shih*) by T'ao Ch'ien was so called merely because the style was thought to be "ancient" even then; and the "new- or recent-style poetry" (*chin-t'i shih*) of the T'ang era—a term designating both the quatrains and the "regulated poetry" (*lü-shih*)—was considered new only with respect to the times. Thus, the plethora of genre names in Chinese poetry quite easily obscures what each of the later genres owes to earlier ones, especially to the style and content found in the two ancient anthologies.

The continuity of this long tradition results from two factors. For one thing, the Chinese written language (*mirabile dictu*) has remained essentially the same—excepting, of course, some peculiarities of usage of grammar in the archaic Chinese and differences in pronunciation from one period of history to another, or from dialect to dialect (but even here a large percentage of rhyme words in classical poetry still rhyme when read in modern Chinese, in one dialect or another). For another, nearly all the poetic devices found in the *Book of Poetry* or in the *Songs of Ch'u*—onomatopoeia, rhyme, alliteration, reduplicatives, or rhymed-compounds,[19] just to name a few—continued to be employed by later poets. What was new, then, with each major genre usually represents those refinements of technique and variations of form which, in an infinite variety of ways, have fostered its growth and, in some cases, its metamorphosis.

A Russian formalist critic, Viktor Shklovsky, has written, "A work of art is equal to the sum of the processes used in it."[20] According to the school of Shklovsky and André Jolles, new art forms are "simply the canonization of inferior (subliterary) genres,"[21] and literature renews itself by "rebarbarization."[22] Though applied to European literature, this genre theory is most apposite if used to explain the development of Chinese poetry. From the very beginning down to the fourteenth century, there have always existed two sources of poetic inspiration, one coming from the people (represented by the folk songs in the *Book of Poetry,* the *tzu-yeh* or folk songs, etc.) and the other from the court or the literati (the two terms virtually synonymous not only because of royal patronage but also because of the Imperial examination). Chinese poetry grew out of the commingling of these two streams, one affecting the other, in many meaningful ways, during the various periods in history. As a musico-literary form, *tz'u* is the most typical product of this kind of cross-pollination.

IV *The Characteristics of Tz'u*

As a literary form, *tz'u* is distinguishable from *shih* in a number of significant ways, both thematically and stylistically. Since spontaneity is the first prerequisite of any lyrical expression, a *tz'u* lyric as a rule carries no subject title, although the "tune title" is always given. (This practice is especially true during the earlier period before the *tz'u* lost its song characteristics and later poets began to provide subject titles or even more explicit explanations of their origin in the form of prefaces.) Then, because of its relative shortness (240 words for the longest of the "tune patterns") when compared with a poem in the "ancient-poetry" style (with indefinite number of lines), it is never used to tell a straightforward story. On the other hand, because of its relative length (anywhere from sixteen to 240 words) when compared with the quatrains (twenty or twenty-eight words) or the "regulated verse" (forty or fifty-six words), with either five or seven words, or syllables, in each line, the extra scope allows the lyrical impulse to be heavily qualified by description or, at times, by a narration of incidents which would be fuller than is possible in a poem of a fixed number of words. (Ignoring the existence of compounds, the Chinese language can be described as "monosyllabic"; hence, I shall use "word" and "syllable" interchangeably. A five-word line is sometimes called a pentasyllabic line; a seven-word line, a heptasyllabic line.) Thus, by this syncretic approach, a lyric poet aims at expressing one's feelings (*ch'ing*) through description, whether it be of events or situation (*ching*) in order to achieve "a fusion of emotion and scene." [23] This constitutes what the Chinese call the poetic "world," the barest outline of which was already discernible in the *Book of Poetry*.

Stylistically, the liberated form of the *tz'u*, the "long-and-short verse" (*ch'ang-tuan-chü*),[24] offers the extreme flexibility of line- and word-arrangement, circumscribed at the same time by numerous refinements of older poetic devices. On account of the varying lengths of the different tune-patterns, later critics arbitrarily decided to call lyrics of under fifty-eight words "small songs" (*hsiao-ling*), those of under ninety words "middle tunes" (*chung-tiao*), and those of above ninety words "long tunes" (*ch'ang-tiao*).[25] Except for some small songs which consist of only one stanza and a very few long tunes which may have three or four stanzas in each, most lyrics consist of two stanzas (strophes), with the second stanza often, though not always, repeating the same line- and word-arrangement as the first. Yet, despite variety in arrangement, all poems in Lyric Meters, when compared with *shih,* are characterized by a greater scope and variety of rhyme schemes and by a greater syntactical freedom within the line, made possible chiefly by varying the place of the caesura in each. The tempo thus achieved is much slower, aided also by such devices as internal rhyme and parallelism, or more properly called antithesis (*tui*), a prominent feature of T'ang poetry. Less specifically, the difference between the two genres lies in something intangible, a kind of "flavor" or atmosphere, which is realized mainly through structural considerations. This is only natural since the technique of *tz'u* composition places the greatest emphasis upon such things as the transition between one stanza and the next, how the lyric ends, and the element of pleasurable surprise concealed in the lines.

To illustrate this difference, I should like to offer, in my close translation, several poems and lyrics written on the same subject of a woman's lament for her absent lover. The first two poems (Poems A and B) are from the sixth century, followed by two quatrains of the T'ang dynasty (Poems C and D) and by a "regulated verse" (Poem E) of the same period. These five poems (*shih*) may be compared and constrasted with the three lyrics (Poems F, G, and H) which follow; two of these are by Wen T'ing-yün of the ninth century, and the last poem is by Hsin Ch'i-chi, written nearly three hundred years later.

Poem A

Boudoir Grief While Looking at a Mirror[26]
by Hsiao Kang (503–551)

Since our parting, I am used to my haggard look;
Others were astounded by my changed complexion.
There is only the mirror of my cosmetics box
In which I can still recognize myself.

Poem B

A Wife's Lament (Written for Someone Else)[27]
by Ho Hsün (*d.* 527)

Sporting swallows return to the corner of the eaves;
Drifting petals fall before my pillow.
But an inch of my heart you cannot see,
As I wipe my tears and pluck at the lute's string.

Poem C

Spring Lament[28]
by Chin Ch'ang-hsü (date uncertain)

Chase the yellow orioles away;
Don't let them cry on the branches.
Their cries only break up my dream
Which then will never reach Liao Hsi.

Poem D

Lament at the Jade-steps[29]
by Li Po (701–762)

The jade steps glisten with white dew;
All night long, it soaks her silk stockings.
Still, lowering the beaded curtain—
Crystal-clear, she gazes at the autumn moon.

Poem E

Palace Lament in Springtime[30]
by Tu Hsün-ho (846–904)

Long ago Beauty dealt me a cruel fate;
Listless before the mirror, I am in no mood for make-up.
When favors are bestowed not upon looks,
Why should I care for my appearance?

The wind is warm, the cries of the birds shatter;
The sun is high, the shadows of the flowers thicken.
Year after year, the girls by the Yüeh Creek*
Will share my memory of the lotus-gathering time.

Poem F

To the Tune of "Lotus-Leaf Cup" (*Ho-yeh-pei*)[31]
by Wen T'ing-yün

One drop of dew, round like a pearl, freezes and chills.
The shadow of the ripples
Fills the pond, the creek.
Green stalks, red blossoms tangle with each other:
My heart breaks;
The water is cool in the gentle breeze.

Poem G

To the Tune of "Dreaming of the South" (*Meng-chiang-nan*)[32]
by Wen T'ing-yün

Thousands, myriads of longings:
I long the most for the one at world's end.
The moon in the mountain knows nothing of the affair of the heart;
The wind upon the water drops in vain flowers before my eyes.
Fluttering, the blue clouds slant.

Poem H

Tune title: "A Big String of Words" (*I-lo-suo*)
Title: Boudoir Thoughts

She dreads to see on the ornamented mirror the single phoenix:
She asks someone to comb her hair.
All spring, she has grieved ceaselessly over the flowers.
How is it, night after night,
The east wind has been so ugly?
She walks around the jade screen, the pearl curtain.
But who is to carry her message?
A jade cup, filled with tears, she raises and holds still:
Afraid that the wine may be just
As weak as his love.

[AL 190]

---

* Referring to Hsi Shih, a beauty of ancient China, who was discovered while washing clothes at a creek near her home in Yüeh before she was brought to the palace.

V *Rhyme Scheme*

Although the distinction of the four "tones"* in the Chinese language, under the two broad categories of "even" (*p'ing,* also translated as "level," meaning "constant in pitch") and "deflected" (*tse,* meaning "not constant in pitch") tones, was made as early as the beginning of the sixth century, and a few private rhyming dictionaries are said to have been written then, the first official rhyming dictionary (*Ch'ieh-yün* by Lu Fa-yen) was not compiled until 601. Nor was this book, enlarged and revised in subsequent editions, adopted as a standard rhyme dictionary until the second half of the eighth century. Hence, early Chinese poets (including Poems A and B above) relied chiefly upon "rhyming by ear," mostly rhyming alternate lines, as will be shown by Poem B in the following romanized text (which will also include a word-for-word pidgin English translation):

yen	*hsi*	*huan*	*yen*	*chi*	
swallow	play	return	eaves	corner	
hua	*fei*	*lo*	*chen*	*ch'ien*	R
flower	fly	drop	pillow	(in) front	
ts'un	*hsin*	*chün*	*pu*	*chien*	
inch	heart	you	not	see	
shih	*lei*	*tso*	*t'iao*	*hsüan* (*hsien*)*† R (*hsien*)	
wipe	tear	sit	pluck	string-of-a-lute	

Capitalizing on the theory of the four "tones"and relying on the sanction of an official rhyming dictionary, the later T'ang poets were able to devise, on the one hand, a rigid prosodic scheme and, on the other, a strict adherence to one rhyme category for all the required rhymed words in a single poem (three such words in a quatrain and four or five in a "regulated verse").[33] The former device, with rare exceptions, insures that groups of words of contrasting tones follow each other, with no more than three words belonging to one of the two tonal groups occurring successively. And the latter insistence on choosing rhyming words, usually limited to words of a "level" tone (exceptions are the "ancient-poetry" or "music-bureau" poems) from

---

*The four "tones" are called "level" (*p'ing*), "rising" (*shang*), "falling" (*ch'ü*), and "entering" (*ju*). The last-mentioned three tones are classified as the "deflected" tones.

† Alternative pronunciation.

one of the 106 categories in the T'ang rhyming dictionary, makes the art of writing a poem a vigorous exercise, especially when a certain category is known to be narrow and contains fewer words than some others. Two of the T'ang poems will be illustrated below by romanized texts (Poems C and E above):

Poem C

| *ta* | *ch'i* | *huang* | *ying* | *erh* | |
| strike | up | yellow | orioles | (diminutive particle) | |

| *mo* | *chiao* | *chih* | *shang* | *t'i* | R |
| do-not | let | branches | above | cry | |

t'i	*shih*	*ching*	*ch'ieh*	*meng*	
cry	time	startle	my	dream	
			(a woman's)		

| *pu* | *te* | *tao* | *Liao* | *Hsi* | R (*ch'i*) |
| not | be-able-to | reach | Liao | Hsi (west) | |

Poem E

| *tsao* | *pei* | *Ch'an* | *Chüan* | *wu* | |
| early | by | Beauty | | deceived | |

| *yu* | *chuang* | *lin* | *chin* | *rung (yung)* | R |
| about-to | make-up | near | mirror | indolent | |

| *ch'eng* | *eng* | *pu* | *tsai* | *mao* | |
| receive | favor | not | be-found-in | looks | |

chiao	*ch'ieh*	*jo*	*wei*	*rung (yung)*	R
ask	me	why	for-the-sake-of	appearance	
	(a woman)				

| *feng* | *luan* | *niao* | *sheng* | *ts'ui* | |
| wind | warm | bird | sound | shatter | |

| *jih* | *kao* | *hua* | *ying* | *ch'ung* | R |
| sun | high | flower | shadow | double-up | |

| *nien* | *nien* | *Yüeh* | *hsi* | *nü* | |
| year | year | Yüeh | creek | girl | |

| *hsiang* | *i* | *ts'ai* | *fu* | *rung (yung)* | R (R: *tung*) |
| mutually | remember | gather | lotus | | |

Rigidity inevitably leads to sameness, but the monotony of rhythm is often circumvented in many ways: by deliberate infraction of rules and appropriate "remedies," or by skillful variation. For instance, it has been noted in many of Tu Fu's (712–770) "regulated verse" poems which require the use of five rhymed words, he deliberately distributes the other three unrhymed words equally among the three groups of the "deflected" tones. As it is also true of Western poetry, in the hands of master poets, rules of prosody have been more honored in the breach than in the observance.

Rigidity also gives way to greater degree of experimentation and freedom with respect to both rhyme and rhythm in Lyric Meters. True, there was, and still is, in use the "Revised Enlarged Rhyme-[dictionary] of Great Sung" (*Ta-Sung ch'ung-hsiu kuang-yün*), issued in 1011; but lyric writers need to reckon with only nineteen broader categories of rhyme words, composed of subgroups which are the equivalent of the traditional 106. But even here, as a Japanese scholar has pointed out, the existence of hundreds of variants of tune-patterns could very well indicate the disdain of many Sung poets for rules and a readiness on their part to create new patterns.[34] Another deviation in the use of rhyme is seen in the increasing use of words in the "deflected" tone as rhyme words and, instead of repetition, in the demand for alternation of rhyming words from one group to the other. I should like to illustrate the rhyme scheme of the tune-pattern[35] in Poem F with the use of lower-case letters to indicate rhyme words in the "deflected" tone and capital letters, the rhyme words in the "level" tone:

The "Tune-pattern" of *Ho-yeh-pei* (23 words, 1 stanza)

i	*tien*	*lu*	*chu*	*ni*	*leng* (R:a)
one	drop	dew	pearl	congeal	cold

po	*ying*	(R:a)
waves	shadow	

mang	*ch'ih*	*t'ang*	(R:B)
fill	pond	creek	

lü	*ching*	*hung*	*yen*	*liang*	*hsiang*	*luan* (R:c)
green	stalk	red	beauty (flowers)	both	mutually	tangle

ch'ang	*tuan*	(R:c)
bowels	break	
(heart)		

shui	*feng*	*liang*	(R:B)
water	wind	cool	

In other words, whereas the rhyme scheme in a "regulated verse" poem would be either $XAXAXAXA$ or $AAXAXAXA$ (X standing for unrhymed words), that of this particular *tz'u* tune would be: a_6 a_2 B_3 c_7 c_2 B_3, which calls for three changes of rhyme and involves rhyme words of both tonal groups.

VI   *Caesura and Over-all Structure*

Both being expressions of emotion, still the shorter *shih* form (Poems A–D) and the equally short *tz'u* lyrics (Poems F–H) differ most noticeably in the way of organization. The quatrains are often praised for their force in developing a single incident in a poem, as if (the Chinese critics would say) "molded in one breath." The last line, then, contains both a surprise and a logical conclusion. On the other hand, the last line of a lyric exhibits a surprise of the opposite kind. As for the "regulated verse" (Poem E), the logical framework is even more noticeable—with the first two lines stating the theme, the next couplet (lines 3–4) continuing or supporting it, another couplet (lines 5–6) giving a new "turn" of thought, and finally the last two lines (lines 7–8) stating the conclusion. At the same time, the middle two couplets (lines 3–6) also serve as the embellishment of the theme.

Within each line of the traditional *shih,* the caesura occurs most often at the end of the second syllable, if it is a pentasyllabic line, and at the end of the fourth syllable, if it is a heptasyllabic line. Of course, there are many excellent lines from T'ang verse which show the most skilful variations of this rule, such as the 1:4 division in a pentasyllabic line or a 2:5 division in a heptasyllabic line. But what are the exceptions in T'ang poetry become the prescribed arrangement in Lyric Meter. And since the lines in a lyric poem may vary in length from one word to ten (or more, depending on the way of counting the extra syllables) words, the variations in the placing of the caesura are inexhaustible. Even as short as a three-word line could be either 1:2 (as in line 4 of Poem H: *shen yeh-yeh,* or "how night-night") or 2:1 (as in the next line: *tung-feng o,* or "east wind ugly"). A six-word line could be 2:4 or 3:3 (with or without parallelism); an eight-word line could be 1:7 or 2:6 or one complete unit without any syntactical break at all. Sometimes, even when two pentasyllabic lines occur together (as in a *shih*), deliberate effort is made to make the first of the two lines a 2:3 division and the next line a 1:4 division, or vice versa.

Since such extreme flexibility is allowed, the one or two extra (occasionally three) words that are used to "lead" the rest of the line (as in a 2:6 or 1:7 division) serve a transitional purpose. Such words may be particles like "furthermore" (*ch'ieh*), "still" (*jen*), or "still more" (*ho-k'uang*) and many others; or they may be verbs like "think of" (*nien*) or "remember" (*i*). As a result, there opens up the possibility of having something like "run-on" lines (as shown in the last two lines in both stanzas of Poem H)—a feature which one Chinese critic has described as corresponding to *enjambment* in English poetry.[36] One cannot help noticing that this characteristic differs markedly from that of the neat, parallel couplets of T'ang poetry. With its use, as we shall see more clearly in Chapter 6, a more discursive style becomes possible, when long and short lines are so juxtaposed as to form virtually verse paragraphs.

VII *Parallelism*

Parallelism, or antithesis (*tui*), a justifiably celebrated feature of T'ang poetry, differs somewhat from the parallelism of Hebraic poetry, as James J. Y. Liu has noted.[37] The most noticeable difference, I think, is that whereas the Hebraic type stresses the contrasting of antonyms ("A false balance is abomination to the Lord: but a just weight is his delight," Proverbs 11:1, King James Version), the words paired in the Chinese parallelism do not have to be antonyms, but contrast-words chosen from the same category of nouns, adjectives, verbs, particles, and so on. In addition, of course, such paired terms must be words of the opposite tonal quality. And in a "regulated verse," this feature is mandatory for the two middle couplets, though occasionally also used in the opening and closing lines as well as the quatrain. An example of this parallelism may be found in lines 5–6 of Poem E above:

| wind | warm | bird | sound | shatter |
| sun | high | flower | shadow | double-up |

It should also be said that this feature is not necessarily an invention of the T'ang poets, as the opening lines of Poem B, written in the sixth century, clearly demonstrate. But its incorporation, as an integral part of the "regulated verse," along with refinements in its use, is the contribution of T'ang poets.

One such technical refinement is to make of this device more than a means of embellishment or reinforcement: in other words, the lines in the couplet must, while satisfying the requirements of tonal contrast and category-pairing, also show a logical connection. This technique is known in Chinese as the *liu-shui tui,* which literally means "running-water parallelism," but could be more accurately translated as "sequential parallelism." An example of this type may be found in lines 3–4 in Poem E above, which show the parallelism of Verb + Noun + Particle + Particle + Noun and also say: "When the imperial favors are not bestowed upon looks,/(what) can prompt a woman to care for her appearance?"

Parallelism as such is less frequently found in lyric poetry; nor is it as rigidly enforced when used; for instance, the repetition of the same word in the paired lines, not allowed in T'ang poetry, is permissible. But when it does occur, as in lines 3–4 of Poem G above, it comes as a surprise. Some tune-patterns, however, demand its use, but with modifications. For example, as described in *The Art of Chinese Poetry,* the tune-pattern of *T'a-so-hsing* ("Treading on Grass") requires not only parallelism in the first two lines of the lyric but also an exact "echo" in the opening lines of the second stanza.[38] Or, instead of being placed so far apart, a line may require what may be called "internal parallelism" (as in line 6 of Poem H above). Or, in a sequence of four lines consisting of one pentasyllabic line followed by three tetrasyllabic lines (5, 4, 4, 4), as in the tune-pattern of "Spring in Princess Ch'in's Garden" (*Ch'in-yüan-ch'un*), the extra first word in the first line serves as the "lead-word" while parallelism is required in alternate lines: line 1 (minus the first word) is paired with line 3, and line 2 with line 4. As an illustration, one lyric in this pattern by Hsin Ch'i-chi contains the following lines:

> Remember that, drinking and sleeping, Magistrate T'ao*
> Eventually achieves supreme happiness;

---

* "Magistrate T'ao" and "Master Ch'ü" refer respectively to T'ao Ch'ien and Ch'ü Yüan.

While being sober all alone, Master Ch'ü
Cannot escape from heavy calamity.

chi	*tsui*	*mien*	*T'ao*	*ling*
remember	drunk	sleeping	T'ao	magistrate
	chung	*ch'üan*	*chih*	*lo*
	eventually	complete	ultimate	happiness
	tu	*hsing*	*Ch'ü*	*tzu*
	alone	sober	Ch'ü	master
	wei	*mien*	*ch'en*	*tzu*
	not	avoid	heavy	disaster

[AL 313]

Thus adapted to the irregular line length of the new meter, an older poetic device is capitalized upon to yield new sources of pleasure: pleasures of recognition as well as surprise.

VIII *Other Poetic Devices*

As a final remark on the characteristics of the *tz'u,* I should like to point out the continuity in the use of various kinds of auditory devices, all of which date back to the *Book of Poetry.* These include alliteration, known in Chinese as "double-sound" (*shuang-sheng*), as seen in "haggard" (*ch'iao-tsui**) in Poem A, or "Crystal-clear" (*ling-lung*) in Poem D, combining ambiguity with alliteration since it could refer to both the crystal screen and the moon, as well as in "fluttering" (*yao-i*) in the lyric (Poem G); reduplicatives as in "year after year" (*nien-nien*) in Poem E, as well as in "night after night" (*yeh-yeh*) in Poem H; and many others.

As conventions grew with the multiplication of tune-patterns, however, there developed two special characteristics worth mentioning. One of these is the repetition of a single word up to three times, such as the "Wrong/ Wrong/ Wrong!" (*ts'o/ ts'o/ ts'o*) at the end of the first stanza, paralleled by "Never/ Never/ Never" (*mo/ mo/ mo*) at the end of the second (in a lyric in the tune-pattern of *Ch'ai-*

---

* *dz'i̯og/dz'i̯äu/ts'iao* and *dz'iwǝd/dz'wi-/ts'uei* in Archaic/Ancient/Modern Chinese (B. Kalrgren, *Grammata Serica Recensa* [Stockholm, 1950], p. 296, p. 134).

t'ou-feng, or "Phoenix Hairpin," written by Lu Yu). Or, there is repetition of successive lines, as in the tune-pattern of "The Ugly Slave" or "The Song of the Eastern Slope," as we shall see in Chapter 6. This kind of device might have helped to provide a dramatic intensity which is otherwise difficult to maintain in a purely descriptive poem.

Emphasis upon description in many lyrics produces the second characteristic of the *tz'u,* which, being vulnerable to imitation, proves to be constrictive at times. By this I refer to the use of poetic epithets such as the compound *lu-chu* in Poem F, or *chin-ch'ien* in Poem H. The literal meaning of the former is "dew-pearl," or "pearly dew," and of the latter, "brocaded-letters," or "letters written on a piece of brocade." In my translations I have tried to distinguish between functional epithets and merely decorative ones. In the former case, I would, at the risk of interpolation, try to communicate its meaning by using the phrase "round like a pearl"; while in the latter case, the intended meaning of the "message" or "letter" should be given rather than the literal translation. In much inferior lyric poetry, there is a heavy dependence upon description for description's sake, without any concomitant emotional content, or musicality, or freshness of insight.

Like any literary genre, lyric poetry in Chinese literature has its golden period as well as its age of decadence. Popular, or vulgate, in origin, it went through the hands of literati-poets in the course of several centuries and became encrusted with all sorts of ancient poetic traditions. Its musical identity rapidly diminished as the poets became interested in developing the linguistic and literary potentialities of the "new" medium—to shape it, as it were, to the ancient ideal of poetry; namely, that poetry must speak of what is in one's heart and "trace emotions daintily." [39]

CHAPTER 3

The Voice of Patriotism:
The "Heroic" Mode in
Chinese Poetry

> Breathes there the man, with soul so dead,
> Who never to himself hath said,
> This is my own, my native land!
> —Sir Walter Scott, *The Lay of*
> *the Last Minstrel,* Canto VI

TO many casual students of Chinese literature, Hsin Ch'i-chi is re-membered (along with his contemporary Lu Yu) only as a patri-otic poet; and to generations of Chinese critics Hsin's lyrics are often linked to those of Su Shih as representative of the grandiloquent, "unrestrained" (*hao-fang*) style of poetry. I propose to examine, in this chapter, the characteristic qualities of several of Hsin's poems distinguished by their "patriotic" fervor, which, for reasons I shall discuss, can be more accurately described as poems in the "heroic" mode. Ostensibly rhetorical, this type of verse touches the most deeply felt sentiments of Chinese readers. By alluding to historical sites and events and to the towering personalities of China's past, it expresses a mixture of longing and despair, combined with admiration or indignation or pity. And by this special use of history, it directs the readers' attention through inference to the present and to the poet's own emotional state rather than merely trying to perpetuate the past.

I *Patriotism and the "Heroic" Defined*

Even without invoking Dr. Johnson, patriotism can be said to be a word which every age, and, indeed, every group, defines differently according to its own beliefs and notions. Its Greek origin (denoting "of one's fathers," and "one's fatherland"), from which is derived the

54

Latin "patriot" or "fellow countrymen," reminds us of shared attitudes of small ancient city-states. In time, the English word came to mean "the character or passion of a patriot, love of or zealous devotion to one's country" (*New English Dictionary*). The corresponding Chinese term *ai-kuo* (lit., "love of one's country") is a compound of modern coinage and has not appeared as a criterion in criticism until recent times. Nevertheless, long before the concept of nationhood in any modern sense developed in China, the general ideas related to patriotism, though referred to in different ways, had been known and cherished for centuries; and it was, furthermore, considered to have a special relevance to poetry.

In premodern China, a term that offers the closest equivalent to the compound *ai-kuo* is the word *chung*. Written with the two radicals, one above the other, of the word for "middle" or "center" (also pronounced *chung*, from which its phonetic value is derived) and of the word for "heart" (pronounced *hsin*)—this word means denotatively "loyalty to the emperor" and, more broadly, "loyalty to a set of higher principles of moral law." To be sure, the quality exemplified by *chung* is regarded as the first of the eight cardinal virtues in Confucian ethics. But Chinese historians are more likely to speak of loyal ministers (*chung-ch'en*) than of loyal poets. Chinese history, too, is replete with the exemplary lives of hundreds of loyal ministers; but fewer of them, I am afraid, are remembered by the average Chinese than the patriots immortalized in fiction or poetry. Clearly, then, there must be an unconscious distinction made between loyalty and patriotism.

A list of historical figures whom the Chinese would consider patriots, even selected in the most random manner, would probably include the following: the poet Ch'ü Yüan, whose advice to the king of Ch'u against an alliance with the state of Ch'in went unheeded and whose death by drowning, in 278 B.C., is still commemorated today in many parts of China with the annual Dragon Boat Festival; the dog-butcher Ching K'o (*d.* 227 B.C.), who was the unsuccessful assassin of the First Emperor of Ch'in; and the general Yüeh Fei, the contemporary of Hsin Ch'i-chi, who died in prison after having been recalled from victorious battles against the Jurchëd. A common theme in the lives of these men is banishment, failure, or persecution; in other words, a thwarted ambition, ambition not for personal glory but to serve the common good of the nation. These men, and not the founding fathers of dynasties, are the "epic heroes" of Chinese literature; their failures—failures on a grand scale—are remembered time and again. As it is fully illustrated in the personal sufferings of Ch'ü Yüan and his poetry—allegorical, symbolic, and prophetic (one thinks of Dante or Blake)—it is the moral grandeur of their tragic failure which is considered by the Chinese to fall within the special purview, or competence, of poetry.

II *The Persistence of the "Heroic" Mode in Chinese Poetry*

To illustrate this special strain of poetic style in ancient Chinese literature, one need not go further back than to the work known as "On Encountering Sorrow" (*Li Sao*) of Ch'ü Yüan, from which I shall quote at random the following lines (in David Hawkes's translation)[1]:

> Eagles do not flock like birds of lesser species;
> So it has ever been since the olden times.   (1. 50)

> The age is disordered in a tumult of changing:
> How can I tarry much longer among them?
> Orchid and iris have lost all their fragrance;
> Flag and melilotus have changed into straw.   (11. 154–55)

> I will follow my natural bent and please myself;
> I will go off wandering to look for a lady.   (1. 166)

Or, one may cite a quatrain of the seventh centrury, entitled "A Song upon Climbing the Yu-chou Pavilion" by Ch'en Tzu-ang (661–702):

> Looking back into history, I cannot see the ancients;
> Ahead into the future, I cannot see the coming generations—
> I think of the everlastingness of heaven and earth,
> And I am desolate and full of tears.[2]

In the opinion of many critics, a consummate expression of this style, blending melancholy with force of expression, is achieved in a lyric by Su Shih. Su's poem assumes that the Red Cliff was where a crucial naval engagement took place between two rivals of the Three Kingdoms period—Ts'ao Ts'ao (155–220), founder of the Wei kingdom, and Chou Yü (175–210, referred to by the latter's courtesy-name of "Kung-chin" in the poem), the strategist for the Sun family who founded the Wu kingdom. Written to the tune of the "The Charm of Nien-nu," the lyric is as follows:

The mighty river flows eastward;
Its surging current has swept away
All the brilliant talented men since ancient times.
West of the old fort, they say, lies
The Red Cliff of the young Chou of the Three Kingdoms.   5
Jagged rocks cleave the clouds;
Fearful surf rends the shores,
Rolling up a thousand piles of snow.
The river and the mountains are lovely as a picture:
How many heroes there were at that time!   10

From this distance, I recall Kung-chin then,
Newly married to the younger Ch'iao sister:
Valorous, handsome, noble, radiant.
With a feathered fan, and wearing a silken cap,
He chats and laughs   15
While the might of the enemy vanishes into smoke and ashes.
My mind strays to the old kingdom:
Like a sentimental soul, I should be mocked
For having my hair flecked so soon with gray.
Life is like a dream!   20
Let me pour one more libation to the moon on the river.[3]

Compare this lyric by Su Shih, written in 1082, with the following written in 1936 by the leader of the proletarian revolution in modern China. The lyric of Mao Tse-Tung (1883-), written to the tune of "Spring in Princess Ch'in's Garden" (*Ch'in-yüan-ch'un*), from which I translate only the second stanza, echoes Su's phraseology as well as his sentiment:

The rivers and the mountains are so full of charm,
Drawing out countless heroes who rival in paying it homage.
I pity the First Emperor of Ch'in and Wu-ti of Han,
Somewhat lacking in literary talent;
And T'ai-tsung of T'ang and Sung's founding monarch,   5
Slightly inferior in poetic gifts;
And Heaven's favorite of one generation,
Genghis Khan
Who knew only how to bend his bow and shoot at buzzards.
All have gone now: 10
To call the roll of the brilliant, talented men,
One still has to look at today.[4]

Without the redeeming quality of genuine emotion, which only an adequate occasion can supply, this kind of verse can sink into a level of bombast and sentimentality, whereas spontaneity and true honesty lifts it to new heights of eloquence. The stance exhibited in the poetry of this order is comparable to much of Byron's, a style which T. S. Eliot has aptly characterized as "semi-Promethean" (and Shelleyan) and partly "Satanic or Miltonic."[5] Eliot calls the "special make-up" of Byron's poetry that "peculiar diabolism, his delight in posing as a damned creature."[6] Byron, according to Eliot, "was an actor who devoted immense trouble to *becoming* a role that he adopted"[7] (italics his). Consequently, he finds in Byron among all the "humbug" and "self-deception" also "a reckless raffish honesty."[8]

Transposed into the Chinese setting and expressed in Chinese terms, these characteristics manifest themselves in the following ways. First, a Chinese poet, whether a literati or a revolutionary, does not have to adopt the role of "becoming" concerned about his country's welfare; by training, a Confucianist likes to think of himself as a man of action who must do his best to benefit humanity at large. Second, more than loyalty to the emperor, a Confucianist must cherish even more zealously his personal integrity; he takes pride (not Satanic, but saintly) in stubbornly adhering to the path of righteousness and adamantly refusing to be tempted or coerced. He tries to save the world; but when the world spurns his efforts, he despises it.

III *Various Qualities Associated with the "Heroic" in Chinese Poetry*

These two fundamental attitudes converge in the concept of a "hero," which is rendered in Chinese either as *ying-hsiung* (line 2 of Mao's poem above) or as *hao-chieh* (line 10 of Su's poem above). These compounds are relatively easy to explain, but they are bound up with other secondary qualities far less explicit. The word *ying* often appears in the earliest literature in the sense of "flowers"[9] but later acquired the meaning of "beauty of talent and character"; while the second word in that compound, *hsiung*, originally meant "the masculine of birds and animals" and hence masculinity, martial valor, or courage. The secind compound for "hero" also consists of two words that complement each other in meaning: *hao* (lit., "possessing greater physical strength than others," or "brave") and *chieh* (lit., "one who is above others in wisdom"). In other words, a Chinese hero must be a man of outstanding sensibility, character, and talent; a man of great courage as well as wisdom; and he is, more likely than not, conscious of his own worth.

Another term significantly related to the concept of a hero, but well-nigh impossible to translate, is *feng-liu* (lit., "wind-flowing"; i.e., the "residual charm," or that which lingers, of a man's general bearing and attitude; referring to one's force of character and connoting something similar to what is conveyed in the word "charisma"). This compound occurs in both of the poems above (line 3 in Su's and line 11 in Mao's), which I have only paraphrased as "brillant, talented men." This compound has a long and curious history: its first occurrence is in *Han Shu*, or *History of the (Former) Han Dynasty*, by Pan Ku (A.D. 32–92), where it is used as a noun to refer to the "general bearing and the spirit" of the people of a region.[10] Toward the third and fourth century A.D., this term came into greater vogue and was used to designate a specific kind of quality, implying dignity and calmness of behavior and nobility of character, including attractiveness in the physical features of a person. One such use occurs in *Chin shu* [History of Chin Dynasty], in the Biography of Wei Chieh (286–312), a man said to be so prepossessing and noble-minded that throngs of people gathered around his house just to have a look at him, so that in the end he died of "overattention and fatigue." At his death, the historian notes, there was a saying that "Wei had been stared to death [*Wei pei-k'an-sha*]."[11] This is the meaning of this compound as it is used in poetry, although one must note in passing another connotation of *feng-liu* (especially common in the current usage of this term) as meaning "characteristic of a gallant, or a gay, pleasure-seeking person." This meaning originated in the eighth century when young scholars visiting the gay quarters of the T'ang capital, Ch'ang-an, were referred to as the *feng-liu* people.

In the idealized portrait of a Chinese hero, another important attribute is spontaneity and freedom from restraint. A hero is unselfish and magnanimous; hence, he is generous with both money and manners. He cannot be concerned with "trivial matters of conduct" (*hsi-hsing*); hence, the quality known as *hao-fang* means "magnanimous and irrepressible." This characteristic appears to carry on the ancient Chinese tradition of knight-errantry (*hsia*, or *hsieh*): the word *hao* occurs in the compound *hao-hsia* (knight-errant) as well as in *hao-chieh* (hero) and in *hao-fang*. Indeed, as James J. Y. Liu notes in his study of *The Chinese Knight-Errant*, "in poetry, it is not always easy to distinguish knights-errant from patriotic warriors on the one hand, and from mere dandies on the other."[12] But, in the context of criticism, the meaning of *hao-fang* is clear: it describes a style which is unrestrained or irrepressible, and which expresses noble (and usually patriotic) thoughts and sentiment spontaneously.

Most Chinese critics of lyric poetry, from the poet's own time down to the present day, speak of Hsin Ch'i-chi as an exponent of the "heroic" style of poetry and as a worthy successor of Su Shih. Two episodes found in the extant records of the poet's career testify to Hsin's reputation among his contemporaries in this regard. In the Preface, dated 1188, to the first volume of Hsin's collected lyrics, the editor Fan K'ai makes the comparison quite explicit by saying:

Many of our contemporaries recognize Master Hsin's *tz'u* to be similar to those of [Su] Tung-p'o. This is not due to conscious imitation; rather, it is because Master Hsin wrote only what he felt in the depths of his heart so that he could not help appearing to be similar to Master Su. Master Su told his disciples that he never wrote under constraint, but only wrote for amusement and pleasure, and in the midst of chatting and laughter. Master Hsin wrote his lyrics in the same manner: if not to amuse himself, it is because he took the greatest pleasure in composition; and if not for pleasure, it is only when he felt relaxed and carefree after wine. . . . He wrote on everything, on rocks and even on the ground, when the spirit moved him. Sometimes he just hummed the verses and did not bother to write them down; sometimes he would burn the drafts he had written. . . . [AL 561]

In the same Preface, Fan K'ai relates Hsin's style to the poet's personality, to his "heroic temperament" (*ch'i-chieh*), to his ambition for public good, and to his desire for a quiet life after retirement. Because Hsin never considered his lyrics as anything but "a tool of self-cultivation," Fan maintains, his works were always characterized by "naturalness and spontaneity." And in the earliest recognition of the diversity of Hsin's style, Fan notes that Hsin's lyrics also included the perspicacious, the pretty, the tender, and the charming—qualities which he finds lacking in Su Shih.

Nonetheless, Hsin Ch'i-chi's predilection for the "heroic" mode overshadows his other styles, and this reputation for the heroic persisted till the end of his career. An event that took place in 1205 (the year of *i-ch'ou*) is described by Yüeh K'o (1173–?1240), a minor poet and the grandson of the famous general Yüeh Fei, as follows:

Chia-hsüan was noted for his *tz'u;* at banquets he would invariably ask the waiting ladies and courtesans to sing what he had written. He was especially fond of the lyric "Congratulating the Bridegroom" [see my *Selected Poems of Hsin Ch'i-chi*] from which he would recite himself the key lines: "When I see green hills full of charm,/ I suspect the green hills,/ Upon seeing me, would find me the same"; or "I bemoan, not that I haven't chanced to meet ancient worthies,/ But that the ancient worthies/ Have not chanced to see me as impertinent as this!" Every time he came to these lines, he would beat the rhythm upon his thigh and ask the guests present for their opinions. . . .

Then he wrote "Music of Eternal Union" [see Poem 8 in this chapter]; its opening lines were "These enduring hills and rivers/ Have left no trace of the hero"; and then there were such lines as "Ordinary lanes and pathways,/ Where people say the royal Chi-nu once lived." He felt the deepest emotion when he came to "A divine chorus of dissonant crows and temple-drums" to the end of the lyric, and he would beat the rhythm himself to the accompaniment of the ladies' repeated singing of these lines. He also liked to insist that guests present point out the shortcomings of his verse. . . . I was young then and forward in my speech . . . and I said, "The last composition we heard is indeed full of heroic sentiments, but the key lines at the beginning and at the end of the lyric sound too much alike. In this new work of yours, I feel that you have used too many allusions." He was greatly pleased with my remark, and, drinking, told those present that I had really discovered his worst addiction. He would change one word or one phrase scores of times, and sometimes he would not finish a composition for several months. . . .[13]

Naturally, the inspiration for heroic thought and sentiment comes from history. In other words, historical truth as the poet sees it is viewed by the Chinese as in some ways irrefutable and, as such, becomes the perfect vehicle for poetry. Hsin's use of the historical material, therefore, deserves close examination so that we might better understand the nature of his response to history, a response which generated such lyrics as those included in this chapter.

IV *The "Heroic" in Hsin's Autobiographical Poems*

Hsin's early career, his political ambition, and the excitement of early military campaigns provided the natural subject matter for some of the autobiographical lyrics written in mid-career and during his last period. A poem specially written for his best friend, Ch'en Liang (Ch'en T'ung-fu), and entitled "A Heroic, or Brave [*chuang*], Song," recalls his soldier's life:

[POEM 1]

Tune title: Dance of the Cavalry (*P'o-chen-tzu*)
Title: A Heroic Song Written for Ch'en
T'ung-fu and to Be Sent to Him
Date of composition: (conj.) 1188

While drunk, I trimmed my lamp and examined my sword;
In a dream, I returned to the strung-out camps and bugle-calls.
My soldiers feasted on roasted flesh of Eight-hundred-*li* Ox;
From fifty-string zithers came a jumble of border melodies.
On autumn's sandy plain, I called the roll.   5

My horse flew faster than the stallion of Liu;
My bow twanged like a clap of thunder.
How I wished to discharge the kingdom's task for my prince
And to win for myself immortal fame!
Yet how sad—my hair turns white!   10

[AL 204]

But it is usually the "long tunes" (*ch'ang-tiao*), popularized by
Su Shih, that are most often used by Chinese lyric poets to express
any sustained feelings on heroic subjects; and the tune of "Full River
Red" (*Man-chiang-hung;* anywhere between eighty-nine and ninety-
four words) has the widest appeal, since the patriotic general Yüeh
Fei (*d.* 1141) once composed a lyric with this tune-title, beginning with the famous line, "My hair in rage bristles against the cap."
For instance, in a poem probably written in mid-career, which begins
with "The Han River eastward flowing/ Has washed clean/ All stench
and blood of the bearded Huns"* [AL 41], Hsin adopted not only the
same variant of this tune (consisting of ninety-three words) as the
one used by Yüeh Fei but also the same rhyme. And he also attempted to echo in his opening line the first line of the lyric by Su
Shih mentioned earlier in the chapter ("The mighty river eastward
flowing").

As a contrast to this style of grandiloquence is Poem 2, which,
although written to the same tune, is a later work; and instead of
ambition and hope, it expresses utter despair and the poet's grief at
his lack of employment. It should be pointed out that a Chinese hero

---

* For a complete translation of this poem, and of other poems which I
quote only in part in this chapter and succeeding ones, see my *Selected Poems
of Hsin Ch'i-chi.*

is never expected to qualify his display of emotion with any apology that his "subdued eyes" are "unused to the melting mood." In fact, the exiled genius of Han Wu-ti's reign, Chia I (referred to in the poem), who died at the age of thirty-three, once memorialized the throne and said, "In viewing the state of affairs of the kingdom, I find there is one thing that could make me cry bitterly, there are two things that make me weep, and there are six things that make me sigh."[14] Hsin's lyric exemplifies this tradition of the self-righteous lament.

[POEM 2]

Tune title: Full River Red (*Man-chiang-hung*)
Title: (None given)
Date of composition: Undetermined

Like the tired Guest of Hsin-feng,
His coat of black fur threadbare,
His eyes full of the dust of the road—
    Tapping at his short sword,
    Hardly three feet of "Blue Snake,"   5
    His brave song broken off:
Doesn't anyone think of a hero growing old south of the river,
Who, if employed, can lift up the Middle Kingdom again?
    How I regret, of poetry and classics,
Ten thousand volumes could not help me to serve the Empire   10
    While the land was sinking!

    Cease from sorrowing over the past:
    Just drown it in Sweet Brew.
    Age comes too easily;
    Joy is never complete.   15
    There is the Beautiful One who pities me
    And puts a yellow chrysanthemum in my hair.
Renounce the hope for tassels of office, a fief of myriad families;
But sell your sword and purchase young calf instead.
    How is it then   20
That in a desolate moment Scholar Chia at Changsha,
    By time's wrong, is moved to tears?

[AL 455–56]

Another poem, written in his late years (after Hsin had been re-activated into service following two periods of "retirement") contains, perhaps, his most mature reflection on his lifelong ambition. In Poem

3, the poet makes no reference whatsoever to any specific event of his career; instead, he juxtaposes his experience of rejection and disappointment with the events of the recorded history. To understand the poem, one must bear in mind its theme, suggested by the place and the time. The name of the pavilion, which was restored by Hsin as the Magistrate of Shao-hsing, is the "Autumn Wind." Emperor Wu-ti of Han (*r.* 140–86 B.C.) had once composed a short song beginning with the line "Autumn wind has risen and white clouds fly!"; and the most famous writer of his reign was Ssu-ma Hsiang-ju (*ca.* 179–117 B.C.), a gifted writer whose elopement with the daughter of a rich man was already legend in Han times. The place is K'uai-chi, in Chekiang, a famous historical site since antiquity: it is supposed to be where the legendary Emperor Yü, who traveled the length and breadth of his kingdom to tame the great flood, died, and was buried. It is also the capital of the old kingdom of Yüeh, during the Warring States period, where a king of Yüeh was defeated by the king of Wu, his archenemy, a defeat which only twenty years later, and after much bitter hardship and preparation, he was able to avenge. In remembering the relationship between Han Wu-ti and Ssu-ma Hsiang-ju, the poet is moved to reflect upon his own fate and the loneliness of his situation, bereft of all comfort except the consolation of the *Records of the Grand Historian* by Ssu-ma Ch'ien (145–86?B.C.), one of Hsin's favorite books. (Other allusions in the poem will be explained in the Notes.)

[POEM 3]

Tune title: Spring in Han Palace (*Han-kung-ch'un*)
Title: Viewing the Rain from the Autumn Wind
Pavilion at K'uai-chi
Date of composition: 1203

Above the Pavilion, the autumn wind blows.
I remember, last year it had, but more gently,
Once before, visited my hut.
The rivers and mountains, everywhere I look, appear strange:
    Yet the scenery is far from indifferent.   5
He who achieves great deeds must retire.
    I feel like the Round Fan
Which in time has grown more estranged from men.
    Blown but not severed—
    The setting sun looks just as before—   10
Over the broad land, there is no trace of tracks of Yü.

For over a thousand years, the song of Wu-ti still survives;
  Yet the poetry of such high romance
  None can savor and emulate except Hsiang-ju.
Only now, all the leaves have shed and the river is chilly.   15
With eyes full of longing, I am stricken with grief.
  A message from old friends:
  "Do not idle and follow the beaten path,
Or forget all about the watercress soup and the sea-perch."
        Who is thinking of me,   20
In the season's first cold night, by the light of a lamp,
Reading a chapter from a book by the Grand Historian?

                                                    [AL 521]

V *Poetry as a Tool for Romanticizing History*

Historical inspiration for Chinese poets emanates from two sources: one from the reading of history; the other from visting places of historical interest. According to a recent study of the use of allusions in Hsin's lyrics, there are one hundred and ten allusions[15] to the *Shih chi* in Hsin's poetry. As would be expected, the majority of these come from the biographies of famous men (fifty-three from "Biographies" and twenty-three from "Hereditary Houses") as against only seventeen from the lives of the rulers.[16] For instance, there are only three references to Liu Pang (247–195 B.C.), the founder of the Han dynasty, as against seven to the life of Hsiang Yü (232–202 B.C.), king of Ch'u and Liu's defeated rival.

Among the colorful figures of the early Han period, however, the greatest number of allusions is made to General Li Kuang (*d.* 119 B.C.) with a total of ten occurrences (followed by Chang Liang, the Marquis of Liu (*d.* 189 B.C.) with nine, and Ssu-ma Hsiang-ju with seven). Li Kuang is said to have been an expert archer and horseman who enlisted in his teens and began fighting the Huns (the Hsiung-nu tribe) in 166 B.C., and who distinguished himself in over seventy campaigns but never received the recognition he deserved. His official biography in the *Shih chi* mentions, for example, his conversation with an astrologer in which he blamed fate for his not having been enfeoffed as a marquis, as had his younger cousin Li Ts'ai, whose talent (he said) could only be ranked "the average of the mediocre,"[17] or the eighth in a scale of nine. Stories about his courage are legion (as will appear in the Notes to the Poems in this chapter). But the greatest irony in his life is that, in the last battle he fought, he was denied his request to lead a battalion against the

Hun chieftain; instead, he was assigned a minor mission which failed when he lost his way. He committed suicide as a means of exonerating his staff officer from blame. It is the life of such a tragic hero which holds for Hsin Ch'i-chi the greatest fascination, and the two poems quoted below illustrate the various ways in which he makes use of the story of Li Kuang.

One way of treating the historical material is to give the bare facts in a straightforward narration. This is done in the first half of the following lyric, which reads almost like a ballad; in the second stanza, the poet makes a deliberate attempt to compare his own situation to the fate of the Han general.

[POEM 4]

Tune title: Divination Song (*Pu-suan-tzu*)
Title: (None given)
Date of composition: Undetermined

General Li of immortal renown,
Stole the horse of a Hun soldier;
His cousin Ts'ai whose talent was below average
Became enfeoffed as a marquis.

Weed the field and pull up old roots;   5
Extend bamboo pipes and add new roof-tiles—
If by chance the Court should reward virtuous farmers,
Who else is there but me?

[AL 400–401]

Contrast this lighthearted approach with the more solemn treatment of the same subject in the next poem, where the more subdued ending describes the poet's own situation with greater emotional intensity.

[POEM 5]

Tune title: Song of Kan-chou (*Pai-sheng Kan-chou*)
Title: Unable to sleep at night, while reading
the Biography of Li Kuang, and remembering the invitation from Ch'ao Ch'u-lao
and Yang Min-chan to join them and
live in the mountains, I, half in jest,
thought of using the allusion to the story
of Li Kuang and wrote this poem to be
sent to them.
Date of composition: Undetermined

The Former General finished drinking, went home at night;
     At the Long Pavilion, he untied the carved saddle.
     Alas, the drunken officer of Pa-ling,
     All in haste, did not know him,
     The taciturn idol of millions.   5
He, on a single mount, shot on a rock thought to be a tiger;
     The stone split at the twang of the startled bow-string—
     Dejected, and never made a marquis;
     Late in years, returning to his farm and garden.

Who is now beckoned by the mulberry and hemp of Tu's Meandering
          River?   10
     Fetching his short coat, his single horse,
     To move his home to the South Mountain?
     See the noble-minded man in sadness and tears,
     Speed his waning years in idle talk and laughter.
          When Han extended her frontier,   15
          His deeds of fame were known far and wide.
          How could it be that even then
     Brave and hearty warriors were also idle?
          Outside the gauze window,
          Slanting wind, fine rain,
          And a siege of slight chill.

                                        [AL 165–66]

     Of course, a more effective use of the historical material is the
metaphoric rather that the literal. In the following lyric, a song of
farewell, allusions are made to four separate historical figures to illustrate the sadness of parting. In the first stanza are the stories of
two women of Han China: Wang Chao-chün ("the tune of *p'i-p'a*"),
who was too proud to bribe a court painter to paint her other than
she looked, and, as a result, was given away in marriage to a Hun
chieftain without the emperor's discovering her beauty until too late;
and Empress Ch'en ("a kingfisher carriage"), who, after losing her
favor with Emperor Wu-ti, succeeded in regaining her position
through a literary composition by Ssu-ma Hsiang-ju. In the second
stanza are the stories of General Li Ling, grandson of Li Kuang,
who ("after a hundred victories") was forced to surrender to the
Huns and remained in captivity while his bosom friend, Su Wu, returned to Han China after nineteen years' imprisonment, also by the
Huns; and Ching K'o ("on the bank of mournful *I* River"), who
undertook the dangerous mission to assassinate the First Emperor of

Ch'in and sang a song of parting, before setting out, at a gathering
in which all the guests wore mourning clothes of white. Unifying the
whole poem is the song of the cuckoo (*che-ku,* also known as *tu-
chüan* or *tzu-kuei*), whose cry is said to mark the end of the spring
season. It is also said that the bird sheds blood in spring and that
the name of *tzu-kuei* is so derived because its cry is homophonous
with *ssu-kuei* (lit., "thinking of going home"). For the irony in the
human situation (parting) and in nature (end of spring), the poet
finds a parallel in the tragic fate of these two men and two women.
And, like Keats's "forlorn" nightingale and "the sad heart of Ruth,
when, sick for home,/ She stood in tears amid the alien corn," the
bird and the historical allusion bring out the despair and the ecstasy,
to achieve a style that is both mournful and grave.

[POEM 6]
> Tune title: Congratulating the Bridegroom (*Ho-hsin-lang*)
> Title: Saying Good-bye to Cousin Mao-chia
> Date of composition: (conj.) 1198–1203

Hear the cuckoo under the green bough.
> But how can one bear
After the partridges' cry has ceased,
> The cuckoo's unrelenting cries—
Crying till spring is all gone, and nowhere to be found,   5
Bitterly lamenting that all flowers are past their prime.
> I reckon nothing equals
> The pangs of parting among men:
The tune of a *p'i-p'a* heard on horseback at the desolate border;
Still more, a kingfisher carriage bidding adieu to the Palace's
> golden gate: 10
> A girl leaving home,
> A concubine sent away.

A general, after a hundred victories, defeated in surrender,
Looking back toward the bridge at home myriad miles away,
And parted forever from his bosom friend.   15
On the bank of the mournful *I* River, the west wind chills:
All who saw him off wore caps and gowns white as snow.
> Just a brave warrior
> Still singing his sad song—
If only the crying bird could know such bitter regret,   20
> I suspect, it would not cry,
> But weep evermore tears of blood.

Who is to join me
In getting drunk under a bright moon?

[AL 429]

Visits paid to ancient sites provide a very common topic in Chinese poetry. The experience allows a poet an occasion not only to reveal his historical sensibility but also to characterize his own emotions, almost as a participant himself in the historical process. Poems of this type may have only innocuous titles which merely indicate the excuse for their composition, but the real theme is usually suggested by the association of the place being visited with the poet's feelings vis-à-vis his own situation. This type of poetry is seen in the following lyric, which describes a visit to a pavilion in Nanking, a city which (as I have remarked before) had been the capital of no fewer than six dynasties during the period of disunion in China following the collapse of the Han empire. The events and the personalities from this period of history—heroes and hermits with their disinterested and noble deeds—are constantly referred to in Hsin's poetry (providing a total of 136 allusions, according to the study by Miss Ch'en).[18] And in the second stanza of Poem 7, the one story about Hsieh An functions somewhat in the manner of an extended or epic simile in English poetry. By this device the poet expresses his grief (in the opening lines) and his fear (in the last two lines), as well as his frustration over the unrealizable fact that either he had not been born in such a time or he was not able to emulate the style of living he found admirable and pertinent to his own day.

[POEM 7]

Tune title: The Charm of Nien-nu (*Nien-nu-chiao*)
Title: Presented to Magistrate Shih Chih-tao,
    upon Climbing Shang-hsin Pavilion
at Chien-k'ang
    Date of composition: 1167–70

I have come to mourn the ancients—
To mount this lofty tower, only to reap
The grief of idle feeling a thousand measures deep!
The "tiger's stance and the dragon's coil" of this once great
    city: where can it be seen?
There's left only a picture of rise-and-fall to fill the eye.   5
Homing birds by river's edge,
Slanting sun beyond the willows,

Tall trees soughing on the dike,
A single sail bent westward:
Whence came the sound of a flute piercing the silence of
        autumn's bamboo grove?   10

All at once I recall the exquisite composure of Hsieh An,
His declining years spent at his Eastern Mountain retreat,
His tears falling at a harpsichord's mournful tune,
Leaving to his brothers and nephews all heroic deeds and fame,
His whole day consumed in a game of chess.   15
    Magic mirror of youth is hard to find,
    Clouds drift on toward dusk:
    Who needs urging to drink another cup?
The gale from the riverhead is mounting in anger,
Morning will see waves and billows tearing at houses.   20
                                                          [AL 11]

VI *History as a Mirror, or the Interpretation of History*

I should like to conclude this chapter on Hsin's response to history
with a poem, composed within the last two years of his life, to illustrate what may be termed a poet's personal approach in the interpretation of historical material. That history can serve as a mirror is not
a tradition exclusive to the West (one thinks of Boccaccio's *De
Casibus* and the Elizabethan work, *The Mirror for Magistrates*);
among the Chinese it is a concept that has been sanctioned since
antiquity. To prove this assertion, one need not go as far back as
the lofty idea of historiography taught by Confucius that the writing
of history is to "confer approbation upon the virtuous and to strike
fear into the hearts of potential rebels and bad ministers." A history
of China produced during the Northern Sung dynasty, by Ssu-ma
Kuang (1019–86), and covering 1,362 years, was given the title
"The Comprehensive Mirror of Perfect Administration," sometimes
translated also as "Mirror of Good Government" (from *Tzu-chih
t'ung-chien* in Chinese); the "Continuation" of this work (*Hsü tzu-
chih t'ung-chien*), by Pi Yüan (1730–97), was compiled during the
Ch'ing dynasty.

Believing that past events have a relevance and moral application
to the present, Chinese poets like to describe their own situation and
feelings by finding analogies in historical events. Thus, in the following poem, the hostility between the Northern Wei (founded by a
non-Chinese tribe) and the weak Southern Sung *kingdom* (to be

distinguished from the Sung *dynasty*, of the poet's time) of the Six
Dynasties period in China is dwelled upon—not only to imply a
parallel between the two periods but also to accentuate the disparity
between hope and achievement, or between illusion and reality.

[POEM 8]

Tune title: Music of Eternal Union (*Yung-yü-yüeh*)
Title: Remembering the Past at Pei-ku Pavilion
in Ching-k'ou
Date of composition: 1205

These enduring hills and rivers
Have left no trace of the hero,
Here in the domain of the King of Wu.
Dance halls and song-filled pavilions,
All romance and charm, have been   5
Beaten by rain, blown by the winds.
Setting sunlight on scrubby trees,
Ordinary lanes and pathways,
Where people say the royal Chi-nu once lived.
Remember those days   10
When golden lances and ironclad horses
Bolted ten thousand miles like tigers.

The debacle of the Yüan-chia era,
Vain as the hope for performing sacrifice at Lang-chü-hsü,
Only to win a retreating emperor's hasty glance.   15
Forty-three years have passed,
Yet I can still recall what I saw:
The road to Yangchow dotted by beacon-fires.
How can I bear to look back?
Beneath the temple of Buddha-fox,   20
A divine chorus of dissonant crows and temple-drums.
Who shall be sent to ask,
"General Lien P'o is indeed old,
But can he really eat a peck of rice?"

[AL 527]

In other words, here the poet is saying that his *personal* past (what
happened on the road to Yangchow) may be compared to "those
days" when the two older kingdoms fought for survival. And where
the founder of that Southern Sung kingdom had once lived, only the
"setting sunlight" now shines upon "scrubby trees" among "ordinary

lanes and pathways." On the other hand, the hills and rivers remain while the heroes of a still earlier period (the King of Wu of the Three Kingdoms period) are gone. It is because the hasty and ill-conceived plans for reconquest, of the earlier ("Yüan-chia") era, had ended in disaster that he is now suspicious of the self-appointed "crows" who beat the war-drums. Although the poet feels that he is not yet too old to serve (the famous general Lien-p'o was dis-qualified on that account), he concludes that since he finds no one to plead his cause, his dream of seeing China reunified will remain for-ever unfulfilled. This, then, is a poem of the deepest gloom and des-pair; and yet, as his discerning young critic, Yüeh K'o, noted, the poem "expresses the most heroic of sentiments."

In analyzing this group of poems which make the fullest use of history, I do not wish to give the impression of suggesting that Chi-nese poets have a "methodical" way of using such materials, or that they decide beforehand what type of historical material can be treated in what manner. Certainly, the literal, the metaphoric, and the interpretative are often found together; and perhaps some other way of classification would be just as satisfactory. It is still further from my intention to imply that Chinese poems of this type are so structured as to contain several levels of meaning in the manner, for instance, of Dante's *The Divine Comedy* (the literal, the moral, the allegorical, and the anagogic). But it will not be amiss, I think, to suggest (without intending any parallel at all) that history was once accorded by the Chinese as much validity, and believed in with as much reverence and rapture, as perhaps the Scriptures were in the West during the Age of Faith. Therefore, for Chinese poets, history is at least capable of being interpreted differently in different periods, or even by the same poet in different poems. By demonstrating sympathy for the events and figures of the troubled past, and by asking in return for the same kind of understanding from its readers, the writers of heroic poetry kept alive the dream that their country might still be free.

CHAPTER 4

The Poetry of a Recluse

> Every discoloration of the stone,
> Every accidental crack or dent,
> Seems a water-course or an avalanche,
> Of lofty slope where it still snows
> Though doubtless plum or cherry-branch
> Sweetens the little half-way house
> Those Chinamen climb towards. . . .
> One asks for mournful melodies;
> Accomplished fingers begin to play.
> Their eyes mid many wrinkles, their eyes,
> Their ancient, glittering eyes, are gay.
> —W. B. Yeats, "Lapis Lazuli,"
> *The Collected Poems of W. B. Yeats*

TO deal adequately with the origin and the development of China's landscape *and* nature poetry, to define their characteristics, to study the principles involved especially in their relationship to Chinese painting, and to speculate (as is so often done) on the similarities and differences with the concept of nature in the Romantic poetry of the West—lies outside the scope of this volume. In this chapter, I shall discuss only the response to nature in the lyrics of Hsin Ch'i-chi; I must begin, however, with a brief summary of the philosophical basis for this type of poetry, with some reference to a few earlier poets, in order to provide for this group of poems their proper historical perspective.

I *China's Landscape and Nature Poetry*

The love of nature manifested itself early in Chinese literature. The two ancient anthologies of poetry, the *Shih ching* and the *Ch'u Tz'u*, abound in references to sun and moon, to curl-grass and plum-trees, to the voice of crickets and the color of the begonia flower, to

iris and lotus, to pepper and orchid, to mallards and doe, and to
birds and animals of all species. But in these unsophisticated songs
the imagery functions chiefly in a metaphoric, or allusive, manner,
as illustrated in the following stanza from the *Shih ching* (in Ezra
Pound's translation).[1]

> White the marsh flower that white grass bindeth
> my love's afar,
>   I am alone.

Enthusiastic response to nature either as a source of pleasure or
as a source of inspiration did not emerge in Chinese poetry until the
post-Han era and did not become significant until the fourth and the
fifth centuries. And when it did, it established, contemporaneously,
two trends known in Chinese as the "landscape" (*shan-shui*; lit.,
"mountains and water") poetry and as the "pastoral," or "nature"
(*t'ien-yüan*; lit., "fields and gardens") poetry. Of course, the distinction between the two terms is rather thin and tenuous, resting
chiefly upon the fact that the former tends to describe nature's
awesome aspects (such as mountain crags and torrents); the latter,
her quieter moods. Critics generally agree that the chief exponent
of the landscape poetry is Hsieh Ling-yün,* the Duke of K'ang-lo
(385–433), a Buddhist by persuasion, who sings of

> Mass of boulders rose from the Twin Streams,
> Waterfalls unfurled from the Three Mountains . . .
> A wilderness of jungle stretched before my eyes.
> I gazed at the crags but could not see the sun.[2]

But the pastoral poet par excellence, admired and emulated by more
later poets than Hsieh, is T'ao Ch'ien, for whom Hsin Ch'i-chi reserved his greatest affection. The poetry of T'ao Ch'ien celebrates
the freedom of the human spirit and the pleasure of gazing at clouds
in the mountains or of drinking wine by the chrysanthemums of the
eastern hedge:

---

* For a study of Hsieh, see Richard Mather, "The Landscape Buddhism of
the Fifth-Century Poet Hsieh Ling-yün," *The Journal of Asian Studies,*
XVIII (November, 1958), 67-79 and J. D. Frodsham, *The Murmuring Stream,*
2 vols. (Kuala Lumpur: University of Malaya Press, 1967).

The air of the hills at sunset is good;
The flying birds in company come back to their nests.
In this is the real savour,
But, probing, I can find no words.[3]

II   *The Eclectic Character of Chinese Eremitism*

The love of nature manifested in Chinese poetry is a product of three different strands of thought which constitute China's intellectual legacy: the Confucianist exaltation of the simple life; the Taoist concept regarding the unity (and the impermanence) of life in the universe and man's subordinate role in the natural world; and the Buddhist teaching regarding Reality and its emphasis upon the search for enlightenment. That these three beliefs can be combined in one person should come as no surprise to anyone even slightly acquainted with the history of Chinese culture; the birth of Neo-Confucianism in Sung China is perhaps the strongest expression of this eclectic spirtit.

Just as bucolic poetry in the West is "rooted" in a "double longing after innocence and happiness, to be recovered not through conversion or regeneration, but merely through a retreat,"[4] the idealization of nature in Chinese poetry is, first of all, a revolt against the corrupt order of society. In China, "the opposite of the *homo oeconomicus*"[5] is not "the shepherd," as in the Western pastoral tradition, but a poor scholar of unquestioned integrity— someone like Yen Hui, Confucius' favorite pupil, whom the Master praised as being able to subsist on "a handful of rice to eat, a gourdful of water to drink, living in a dilapidated alley, and to show at the same time cheerfulness of disposition."[6] Or, he could be a non-compromiser, on political and ethical grounds, like the legendary Po-i and Shu Ch'i, described in *The Analects* as the "lost" or "fleeing" people (*i-min*)[7]—two brothers who fled to the mountains to live on thorn-ferns rather than eat the grains of the new dynasty of Chou, and later died of starvation. What the Confucianists call the *i-shih* ("the scholar who fled") is later more widely known, with Taoist connotation, as *yin-shih* ("one who withdraws or retires"), often translated as "hermit" or "recluse."[8] Especially in times of turmoil or political misrule, scholars see a greater benefit in seeking the pleasures of the pathless woods and in refusing to "herd with men."

III *Taoist Quietude and Buddhist Enlightenment*

While Confucianism merely recognizes the virtue of withdrawal from the world, it is philosophical Taoism which explicitly defines man's proper course of action in his relationship to the natural world. According to the teachings of the *Tao-te-ching* (*The Book of the Way and Its Power*), ascribed to Lao Tzu, and of the writings of Chuang Tzu (*ca.* 369–286 B.C.), the ruling principle of the universe is the "nameless Tao," unchangeable and constant, a Void to which everything owes its being. Only two operative laws are discernible, the Taoist philosophers maintain, and they are "the reversal of things" ("When a thing reaches one extreme, it reverts from it") and *wu-wei* (lit., "non-action," or 'having-no-activity,'"[9] sometimes translated as "actionless activity"),[10] which means that one must do nothing that is contrary to one's nature. "A sage does nothing by which everything is done"; and only by emulating the model of spontaneity and naturalness, doing away with all artificialities and distinctions (out of which human desires are born), can one find survival or happiness in the world.

The Taoist emphasis on achieving equanimity, or quietism, and on recognizing the principle of impermanence in the universe leads to a state of submerging one's self in the totality of experience. Thus, the natural world in the poetry of such great Chinese poets as T'ao Ch'ien or Wang Wei can often achieve what has been described by a twentieth-century Chinese critic as the "selfless" (*wu-wo*)[11] state of human experience in poetry. But, whether or not a poet can realize such an ideal, his approach to nature is always characterized, not by a sense of awe, but by affection; not to see nature as an external order of things, the manifested Creation, but as something that is serene and joyful, despite, or because of, its transience. The "moment" that "abides," even though it is not due to human striv-ing—and precisely because it is not—is the fairer when one knows that it will pass. "Beauty that must die," an English poet has written, can be seen by "none save him whose strenuous tongue/ Can burst Joy's grape against his palate fine"; William Butler Yeats, with the eye of a painter, tells us that the eyes of a Chinese artist that look on avalanches and plum-flowers, "their ancient, glittering eyes, are gay."

In the history of Chinese thought, this emphasis on quietism, in-culcated by the Taoists, has been reinforced by "Chinese Buddhism," [12] known in China as the *Ch'an,* or Meditation, school (better known to the West by its Japanese name as Zen Buddhism), a doctrine which has been described by a contemporary Chinese philosopher as "the synthesis of Indian Buddhism with Taoism." [13] The Chinese word for "nature" is *tzu-jan,* (lit., "thus-so"). Hence, the Buddhist teaching concerning the Reality of all sentient things in the world and the need for Enlightenment holds no incongruity with philosophical Taoism. Hsin's poetry contains far fewer references to Buddhism than to the ideas of Taoist philosophers. (This will be discussed further in Chapter 6.) It is important, however, to recognize the indistinguishable wholeness of Chinese philosophical tradition: Buddhist teachings have been absorbed into philosophical Taoism, and the latter has been made compatible with Confucian tenets.

IV *Hsin's Response to Nature*

This wholeness of approach can be seen most dramatically in Hsin Ch'i-chi's response to nature. While the essentially Taoist philosophy he espoused is derived from the teachings of Lao Tzu and Chuang Tzu (see Chapter 6), he chose for his poetic model the poetry of T'ao Ch'ien whom he more than once addressed as "my teacher." Like the recluse-poet, the "Master of Five Willows," Hsin was driven from public office by his unbending character; and he found in the more enduring world of the landscape and the seasons not only comfort and joy but also a source of poetic creativity. Although he never achieved, in life as well as in his works, the complete nonattachment of T'ao Ch'ien, he responded to nature's beauty and beneficence with as genuine a rapture and wrote about the simplicity of the pastoral life with as much insight. On the simplest level, this response is revealed in the imagery he derives from nature, which I propose to examine first before I deal with the more complex poems with themes suggested by objects of the natural world. This group of poems is rather large and will be discussed under three headings which I shall call the Tensional Aspect, the Concrete, and the Universal.

V *Nature Imagery*

Images derived from nature are perhaps the commonest feature of Chinese poetry: they occur in the poetry of all ages, in the works of the highest flights of imagination as well as in the most hackneyed lines produced by rhymesters of every village in China. The beauty of moonrise is believed to sharpen the pangs of separation; the waxing and waning of the moon suggest the cycle of joy and sadness; the regularity in the migratory habit of wild geese is associated with the anxiety of waiting for a message from loved ones (the formation of wild geese in flight resembles the Chinese character for "man"); the plucking of a branch from the willow tree is a symbol of parting; the annual return of swallows is a reminder of the departure of guests; and so on. Sanctioned by centuries of usage, these comparisons, when they occur for the thousandth time, no longer excite the imagination as they once did as novel figures of speech. Particularly in lyric poetry, this kind of imagery abounds, along with isolated compounds, or poetic epithets, such as "autumn waves" (*ch'iu-po*) for the eyes of a woman; "cloudy hair," or "cloud-like hair" (*yün-fa*) for a woman's hairdo; and the like.

Hsin Ch'i-chi, in his voluminous works, is sometimes guilty, but no more than any other lyric poet, of overusing these expressions. For instance, what is quite apparent in the following lines is a certain triteness, or even absurdity in these metaphors, especially in the last three words: *ti meng-hung* (lit., "drip dream-soul"):

> With tears in my eyes, I see you off, and
> they pour down like rain;
> I do not wish to pluck the overhanging willow;
> I ask only that my grief follow you as you leave. . . .

[AL 104]

> My homeward thoughts are like tangled clouds;
> Since spring I have come to hate the twilight—
> Intolerable is the rain coming down from the eaves at dusk,
> I shall wait for tonight when the soul in my dream drips
> again. . . .

[AL 86]

But, commonplace as these expressions are, they sometimes challenge the poet to add a new twist to the hackeyed clichés. In addition to the "autumn waves" already mentioned, a woman's eyebrows are frequently compared to "distant hills" (*yüan-shan*).[14] In the following lyric, a product of fancy more than anything else, the poet makes use of all the traditional metaphors found in a poem on parting, to create a type of conceit in which the "tenor" and the "vehicle" are reversed:

[POEM 9]

Tune title: Foreign Boddhisattva (*P'u-sa-man*)
Title: (None given)
Date of composition: Undetermined

All the west wind brings is travelers' regret!
The horse's head senses with joy the approaching date of return.
 I try to climb the small red pavilion;
 But the flying geese, one after another, spell the word grief.

Where I lean against the railing, in my idle mood,   5
There's only an endless stretch of innumerable hills—
 They do not resemble your eyebrows aslant;
 Nor are they as bright as your eyes.

[AL 86]

In the more successful poems, Hsin frequently shows the ability
either to endow the inanimate objects of nature with human emotional attributes or to associate an experience in the natural world
with poetic creativity. The first of these two characteristics can be
seen in several of the longer poems included in this chapter; a
typical example is the following stanza from a lyric written upon
recuperation from an illness in autumn:

My pillow and mat, in this hall by the creek,
 first feel the touch of autumn's chill;
Sundered clouds, coursing above the river,
 are gathered up at dusk.
Red lotus flowers, leaning each upon each,
 appear as if drunk;
The white birds, all silent, must be
 communing with their private grief.

[AL 153]

The second characteristic may be observed in such lines as
"Beyond the willows I search for spring,/Alongside the flowers
I find a line of my verse" [AL 69], or "When a line of my song
reaches the plum blossoms,/Spring breeze is felt in thousands
of homes" [AL 271]. The following poem, which illustrates the
different ways of organizing nature imagery mentioned above, is
emotional, philosophic, and intense as well as verbally dexterous:

[POEM 10]

Tune title: River Fairy (*Lin-chiang-hsien*)
Title: Sending My Cousin [Hsin] Yu-chih Off
to Fu-liang
Date of composition: Before 1188

Temple and Court, hills and forest, all are stuff of dreams;
The world's praise or shame is nothing to be startled at.
If only one could be at peace and live out this life—
    A wine-cup in autumn to draw in the dew,
    Lines of verse at night to trim the ice!   5

I remember the night of wind and rain, by a small window,
Our beds facing each other by the lamplight, how happy we were!
I ask, who is to accompany you on this trip of a thousand miles?
    Hill in the dawn like penciled eyebrows,
    And autumn river bright as a mirror.

                                [AL 169]

VI *Complex Poems about Nature: The Tensional Aspect*

In Hsin's collected works there is a large group of autobiographical poems descriptive of his villa at Ribbon Lake or recording impressions of his frequent outings to places of scenic beauty. These lyrics reveal not just the physical beauty of the landscape, or merely the mood and the activities of a poet as a recluse. Rather, they express the tension created between the joy of an unencumbered life in the presence of nature and a lingering sense of Confucian responsibility. In those poems presenting an idealized picture of the life of a recluse, T'ao Ch'ien is frequently mentioned. For example, in one poem (to the tune of *Ch'in-yüan-ch'un*) entitled "On the Eve of the Completion of My New Villa on Ribbon Lake," Hsin begins with the line "Three Trails now ready" alluding to T'ao's well-known domicile. Chrysanthemum by the eastern hedge, the symbol of T'ao's detached mind, is alluded to again and again, as in the following: "By the eastern hedge I must plant much chrysanthemum/And learn from Yüan-ming,/Though in pleasure for wine or inspiration for poetry I am not his equal" [AL 118]. The next two lyrics, Poems 11 and 12, typically reflect the excitement and the tranquility, the tumult and peace, which Hsin must have felt in nature's presence.

[POEM 11]
>   Tune title: Prelude to Water Music (*Shui-tiao ko-t'ou*)
>   Title: Swearing an Alliance with Sea Gulls
>   Date of composition: 1182

>   Ribbon Lake, how much I love your company!
>   The overspreading gleam, as from a jeweled box flown open!
>   The Master, save for his staff and shoes, is idle;
>   He walks there a thousand times in one day.
> All of you sea gulls, my companions by this sacred oath: 5
> From this day on, after we have plighted our friendship,
>   I ask you not to be suspicious of my company.
>   Where is the white crane?
>   I invite her to join you in coming hither.

>   Let me break up the green duckweed,   10
>   Push back the lush algae,
>   Stand on the emerald green,
>   To peep at fish and laugh at their naïve scheming,
>   Who cannot understand why I lift my wine-cup.
> Forsaken pond, desolate hills of long ago;   15
> A bright moon, clear breeze—this night:
>   In a lifetime, how many alternations of grief with joy?
>   The eastern shore still lacks a little shade;
>   I need to plant some more willows.

>   [AL 99]

[POEM 12]
>   Tune title: Partridge Sky (*Che-ku t'ien*)
>   Title: Written at the Po-shan Monastery
>   Date of composition: (conj.) 1198

>   I did not take the road to the Capital:
>   Instead, I made mountain monasteries tired of greeting me.
>   Where lay the unflavored, among flavors, I sought my joy;
>   Midway between the useful and the useless, I passed my life.

>   I would rather be myself: 5
>   Why pretend being someone else?
> Having been everywhere, one always returns to farming.
>   One pine, one bamboo, is a real friend;
>   Mountain birds, mountain flowers, are my brothers.

>   [AL 136]

VII   *Complex Poems about Nature: The Concrete or Objectified Aspect*

Seasons, festivals, or specific plants and flowers constitute another group of recurrent themes in Hsin's poetry. In these lyrics it is usually a single, concrete aspect of nature that is dwelled upon, allowing the poet to oppose his minute observation of nature with his interpretation of the unchanging law of the universe. In Poem 13, for example, the poet begins by evoking spring's more tranquil mood which, quickly and imperceptibly, lapses into its more somber aspect and inevitably conjures up the sorrows of the human predicament. In this poem of eight lines, the poet uses the word for "spring" (*ch'un*) four times, the word for "wind" (*feng*) twice, the word for "flower" (*hua*) twice, and the word *jen,* or "man" (translated as "I," line 6, and "loved ones"), also twice. And, by means of this conscious variation and repetition, the poet reveals not only his own susceptibility to nature but also his austere conviction that old age and loneliness of separation are as certain as the fragileness of spring.

[POEM 13]
Tune title: Spring in Jade Pavilion (*Yü-lou-ch'un*)
Title: (None given)
Date of composition: Undetermined

I wish to plead with the wind to let fine spring tarry;
Spring, dwelling south of the city along the flower-strewn road,
Has not yet followed the flowers drifting down to water's edge;
But is there, where willow catkins scatter down to sodden ground.

Each fleck of white in the mirror tells me of what I've missed.   5
I have not wronged spring, spring only wrongs itself.
Dream vanishes, loved ones far away: that much grief
Dwells where wind and rain beat down on the pear-blossoms.

[AL 482]

Sometimes, the description of nature is so intense and vivid that traditional Chinese scholars (who cringe at the thought that fine poetry could be produced from trivial subject matter) like to interpret allegorically what is simply a poem on the seasons. For example, in one lyric entitled "On the First Day of Spring" (to the tune of *Han-kung-ch'un*), Hsin writes:

Spring has returned!
Just look at spring's streamers and ribbons*
Gracefully dancing on pretty maidens' heads.
Alas, the indiscriminate wind and rain
Yet reluctant to store away the lingering cold!
Seasonal swallows,
I imagine, will this night
Dream of returning to their orchard,
Though unprepared to scent
The golden tangerines that go with wine
Among green leeks and scallions piled on the plate. . . .

[AL 463]

And a modern critic theorizes that the deliberate juxtaposition of the "golden tangerines" and the "green leeks and scallions" contains the poet's rebuke of Prime Minister Han T'o-chou because of the latter's inability to distinguish talented ministers from sycophants.[15]

Poems 14 and 15, as their titles indicate, belong to a subgenre of Chinese poetry known as the "descriptive-of-things" (*yung-wu*) poems. Adapted to the *tz'u* meter and growing increasingly popular toward the end of the Southern Sung period, this type of composition started as a literary exercise, somewhat in the manner of the "rhyme-prose" (*fu*) of the Han era. Usually, the subject is either a plant or a bird; and because of the random nature in topic selection and the narrowness of the prescribed topic, the poet is required to rely upon a certain ingenuity if he desires to say something fresh and original.

The subject of both Poem 14 and Poem 15 is the plum-blossoms, or *mei*, the blossoms of the earliest flowering tree in China. (*Mei*, or "plum-tree," which flowers before the winter is over, is to be distinguished from *li*, which bears edible fruit.)In Poem 14, Hsin again reverses the "tenor" and the "vehicle" and views the course of spring through a human situation. Suggested by the fragile beauty of the plum-blossoms, the expectation of spring is likened to the

---

* The text reads: *ch'un-fan* (lit., "spring pennants"), referring to hair-ornaments cut from colorful papers and worn by gentlewomen of the Eastern Capital, or K'ai-feng, on the first day of spring. See Meng-Yüan-lao (*fl.* 1126), *Tung-ching meng-hua lü* [Recollections of the Splendor of the Eastern Capital], 1147 (Shanghai, 1956), p. 172.

naïveté of a young girl, while the profligate and extravagant nature
of spring, to the grief of a deserted woman—implying that grief is
known only by those who have seen spring depart. Thus, howsoever
insignificant, an object of nature is seen in all its intimate relationship with the human world and made to reveal a spiritual reality.

Poem 15 again illustrates how Hsin successfully integrates the
description of natural scenery with the delineation of human emotion.
In the first three lines, the poet evokes all the details of the cold
season—wild geese* (also suggestive of letters), frost, the moon
unaccompanied, except for the thin clouds which are left with the
job of "protecting" and "cherishing" (both meanings are implied in
the word *fu*) her, and the thin, first ice of the season—to accentuate
the plum-blossoms' fragile beauty and her loneliness (when no other
flowers are blooming). Then, in line 4, with the use of a striking
metaphor *hsi-lien* (lit., "the brook [and] a lady's dressing or cosmetics box"), the poet accomplishes the transition to the human
world; and the comparison of the subject with a young girl who shuns
all artificial aids and makeup is brought to a close only with the end
of the first stanza. And it is only in the second stanza when the emotional involvement of the poet begins—and begins startlingly with the
chi-mo ("lonely" or "forlorn"). This now human situation is sketched
lightly by a series of loosely parallel lines. Thus, in the next line (line
19), even the conventional epithet *lin-hung* (lit., "scaled-fish and
wild geese," meaning "letters" or "message"; hence, "courier") does
not appear out of place in Chinese since the human experience of
loneliness and desertion continues in the next three lines to be
sketched by means of references to the natural world. Of course,
such references as the "butterflies" and "peach-trees and willows" are
used to describe the wantonness of spring which, by contrast, brings
out the unique charm of the plum-blossoms. The analogy, thus completed, ushers in the concluding thought of the last three lines, that in
the human world it is more a matter of grief to be listening to the
sound of the post horn as a boat leaves the shore (with the words
leng-lo, or "desolate," echoing the *chi-mo* of the first line of this
stanza).

---

* See note to line 1 of Poem 15.

[POEM 14]
Tune title: Butterflies (*Fen-tieh-erh*)
Title: On "Fallen Plum-blossoms," and Replying
to a Poem Sent by Chao Chin-ch'en
Date of composition: 1200

Yesterday's spring was like
A thirteen-year-old girl learning to embroider:
Branch after branch,
She never sketched the blossoms thin.
Then, callously,   5
Came down hard
Reviling wind and rain
Upon the garden
To carpet the ground in wrinkled red.

And now spring is like   10
A frivolous youth hard to keep home.
Remembering last time
Bidding spring goodbye,
Churning spring waves
All into wine,   15
A river of heady brew—
She invites the unsullied grief
To wait for her by the willow bank.

[AL 403]

[POEM 15]
Tune title: Auspicious Immortal Crane (*Jui-ho-hsien*)
Title: On Plum-blossoms (*Fu-mei*)
Date of composition: 1191–94

The cold of autumn's frost pierces through the curtain
When light clouds are sheltering the moon:
New ice still thin,
Before the mirror brook she combs her hair;
Then thinks of dallying with scent and powder,   5
But seductive art is hard to learn.
Pale and thin, her flesh,
Fold upon fold
Of colored silk, her foil.
Relying on the east wind—   10
One pleasant smile from her,
In a wink, ten thousand blossoms fall in shame.

Forlorn!
What place can be called her home?
Garden after a snow,   15
Pavilion by the water's edge,
Or an ancient assignation in Fairyland.
        Yet whom can she send
        As her courier?
Butterflies care only   20
To chase after peach-trees and willows;
The southernmost boughs laden with flowers, they do not know.
        Still her heart would grieve
        On some desolate evening
At the scattered sounds of the post horn.   25

                                                [AL 280–81]

VIII   *Complex Poems about Nature: The Universal Aspect*

In the last group of nature poems, Poems 16–19, all dealing with
the less localized aspects of nature, the "complexity" takes on the appearance of complete artlessness and simplicity. Just as the Taoist
canon, the *Tao-te-ching,* has prescribed that the greatest wisdom appears like stupidity, these simple lyrics achieve a high level of artistic success because the skill of the poet is hidden and unobtrusive.
Here the descriptions of nature do not serve merely a decorative
purpose, as they do, for instance, in Poem 9, which stands at the other
end of the scale as an example of inventive craftsmanship. In these
poems the poet contents himself with sketching a rustic scene, often
coupled with an ordinary human situation; and the style so achieved,
a quality that is unadorned and dispassionate, is much prized by Chinese poets. It is often referred to by the critical term of *p'ing-tan,*
which carries a dictionary meaning of "plain, flat, or tasteless," but
really denotes "that which never cloys or satiates"; hence, utter simplicity. Probably, the effects created by these poems are comparable
to what is achieved in the best of Sung monochrome paintings done
in the style of *pai-miao* (lit., "plain or unadorned sketching"). Or,
to put it in the language of Keatsian poetics, these poems make no
"palpable design"[16] upon their readers; and they may have come close
to the quality Keats attributes to all great poetry. "Poetry," he says,
"should be great and unobtrusive, a thing which enters into one's
soul, and does not startle it or amaze it with itself—but with its subject."[17]

[POEM 16]

Tune title: Pure Serene Music (*Ch'ing-p'ing-yüeh*)
Title: Life in the Village
Date of composition: Before 1188

Thatched eaves, low and narrow;
Grass all green by the creek—
Happy with wine, the Wu dialect sounds lilting to my ear:
I wonder whose grandparents are these white-haired ones?

The oldest son hoes bean east of the creek,   5
The second boy mends the chicken coop.
I love best the youngest crafty child:
He lies by the creek breaking open lotus-pods.

[AL 190]

[POEM 17]

Tune title: West River Moon (*Hsi-chiang-yüeh*)
Title: Traveling the Yellow Sand (Huang-sha)
Road at Night
Date of composition: 1186–87

Startled magpies scurrying from the branches in the moonlight,
The chittering of cicadas in midnight's cool breeze;
Talk of a bountiful year, in the fragrance of ripening grain—
The loud croaking of frogs assails my ears.

Seven or eight stars on the far horizon,   5
Two or three drops of rain closer by the hill—
A familiar wineshop by the woods beside the shrine
Appears suddenly as the road winds past the bridge.

[AL 250]

[POEM 18]

Tune title: Partridge Sky (*Che-ku-t'ien*)
Title: On the Road to Yellow Sand (Huang-sha)
Date of composition: Before 1188

A line of my verse is trimmed and shaped by spring breeze;
Hills and streams unroll a vista like a painting.
Light-limbed sea gulls glide away on phantom boats;
Shaggy dogs turn back to greet a country woman coming home.

Bamboo and pine,   5
A mass of green,

Seem bent on lifting the last of snow to vie with the beauty
        of sparse plum-blossoms.
But, alas, the jumble of crows, clumsy and witless,
Time and again, kick the crystals down!

                                [AL 250]

[POEM 19]
            Tune title: The Prickly Pear (*Shen-ch'a-tzu*)
              Title: Visiting Rain Cliff (Yü-yen) Alone
                  Date of composition: 1182–88

I stroll along the stream and follow my shadow;
The sky lies at the bottom of the clear stream.
In the sky above are drifting clouds;
Among the drifting clouds, I find myself.

Who's there to harmonize my soaring song?   5
From hollow valleys, pure notes rise.
Not from spirits nor from immortals—
Just a song of peach-blossoms from a crescent stream.

                            [AL 142–43]

CHAPTER 5

The Poet as Craftsman

> As a form of competition proper, archaic poetry is barely distinguishable from the ancient riddle-contest. The one produces wisdom, the other words of beauty. Both are dominated by a system of play-rules . . . [and] both presuppose a circle of initiates who understand the language spoken. . . . Only he who can speak the art language wins the title of poet.
>
> —Johan Huizinga,
> *Homo Ludens*

ON the assumption that the many aspects of Hsin Ch'i-chi's style as a lyricist are the result of his conscious craftsmanlike concern for his art, I wish to examine in this chapter the more technical side of his composition, beyond what has been discussed in Chapter 2. Specifically, I should like to note new departures in stylistic emphasis, when compared with the lyric poetry of earlier periods, and to call attention to the diction, the meter (which is discussed in the Notes to this chapter but will not be considered in the text[1]), and the imagery peculiar to Hsin's verse. (Hsin's use of allusion will be dealt with separately in the next chapter.) On the whole, Hsin's response as an artist in the manipulation of the new form is characterized by (1) his keen interest in experimentation; (2) his preference for, and mastery of, the "long tunes"—a practice made popular by Su Shih; (3) his fondness for the use of allusions; and (4) his versatility, resulting in a variety of stylistic effects—which range from unusual simplicity and plainness to great intricateness and delicacy, from colloquialism and humor to an extremely complex and erudite use of the language. Of necessity, I shall on occasion cite isolated passages out of context, but where an entire poem is necessary to elucidate an aspect of technique or form, I will render the complete translation (and transliteration of the original).

I *The "Hua-chien" Style*

Over two hundred years had elapsed between the publication of the first *tz'u* anthology, known as the *Hua-chien chi* [Among-the-Flowers Collection, Preface dated 940], and the time of Hsin Ch'i-chi. The work consists of close to five hundred lyrics by eighteen poets of the ninth and tenth centuries. And in language that is generally elegant, employing predominantly the shorter tunes, the poets represented in this collection attempt a style both unique and far-reaching in its influence upon the *tz'u* of later centuries. By a series of metaphors, the editor of this volume, Ou-yang Chiung (896-971), who also contributed thirteen lyrics, described its content as being "like carved jade to excel nature's cunningness [*ch'iao*], or like a branch of flowers, trimmed in such a way as to rival in loveliness [*hsien*] the gorgeous [*yen*] colors of spring."[2] The subject matter, also, is more or less uniform and confined to the depiction of romantic love. To the delineation of such feelings as ennui, loneliness, or the grief of parting and separation, the poets carefully subordinate all descriptions of scenery and the imagery drawn from nature as well as the world of art for descriptive purposes. Poems F and G, included in Chapter 2, are characteristic of the style of these poets, which continued to be imitated by lyricists in succeeding generations until the present day. Another example from this collection, to be referred to again in this chapter, is the following lyric by Chang Pi (*fl.* 940):

To the Tune of "River Message" (*Ho-ch'uan*)[3]

Red almond blossoms
Reflect each other's beauty from entwined branches;
     In the misty rain,
One courtyard's emblazonry leans against the east wind.
     The fragrance dissolved   5
     Penetrates the curtained window.

The setting sun seems to be whispering to spring light;
     Butterflies frolic and dance—
Making even the orioles trail their notes in envy.

My soul melts away in front of the jade goblets,   10
  To where the immortal goddess
By the Jasper Pond lies drunk, as dusk descends.

Heavily descriptive and seemingly frivolous, the lyrics composed in this style depend chiefly upon their sensory appeal, implicit in the imagery, to achieve a consistent tone. And the accumulation of details is often so overpowering that it drives home an argument never explicitly stated. Hsin's poem, "Lantern Festival" (to the tune of *Ch'ing-yü-an*),* may be seen as an example of this descriptive mode—containing references to the four senses of sight, hearing, smell, and touch, and, at the same time, fusing the four worlds of reality, art, nature, and history (in the allusion used) into a love song.

The "boudoir lament" type of poetry, a hallmark of the *Hua-chien* collection, is not often regarded as akin to Hsin's style as a lyricist; nonetheless, a number of lyrics written in this vein (one of which was introduced in Chapter 2) could rival the best of the *Hua-chien* anthology. The following lyric, in which the speaking voice is assigned to a woman, demonstrates the poet's mastery of the *Hua-chien* style, especially in his brillant use of the repeated refrain to add to the emotional intensity.

[POEM 20]
                Tune title: Song of the Eastern Slope (*Tung-p'o-yin*)
                        Title: Boudoir Lament
                Date of composition: Undetermined

        Her delicate fingers pluck an ancient lament,
          Deftly tap on the embroidered board;
      With a clear song, her eyes trail the geese in the west wind
          Until their formations break off, her word blown away.
          Until their formations break off, her word blown away.   5

        Deep in the night, she makes her prayer to the moon
          West of the carved window,
          Only the shadow of the cassia tree
          Fills the empty stairs.
      A kingfisher curtain conceals her, and no one near—   10
          Her silken garments twice as loose.
          Her silken garments twice as loose.

                                                        [AL 504]

___

* See my *Selected Poems of Hsin Ch'i-chi.*

II *Parody, Imitation, and "Re-creation"*

In addition to these shorter lyrics, I should like to introduce two
other poems unmistakably related to the *Hua-chien* style. The first
(Poem 21), as indicated by the title and the tune title, was written,
not improbably, as a parody of two poems of Chang Pi's in the
"Among-the-Flowers Collection." Both written to the tune of the
"River Message,"⁴ one of these ("Red almond blossoms") was quoted above, and the other begins with the line "How vast is the water
under the clouds" (*miao-man yün-shui*). In Hsin's parody, the deliberate juxtaposition of the poetic language with colloquial expressions
(such as "over there," or *na-pien*), seems to show the poet's weari-
ness with the proliferation of conventions in love poetry—somewhat
like Shakespeare's Sonnet 130:

> My mistress' eyes are nothing like the sun;
> Coral is far more red than her lips' red;
> If snow be white, why then her breasts are dun . . .

which effectively parodies the use of conceits in the Elizabethan son-
neteering convention.

[POEM 21]

　　　Tune title: (T'ang) River Message (*T'ang-ho-ch'uan*)
　　　　　Title: In Imitation of the *Hua-chien* Style
　　　　Date of composition: Undetermined

　　　Spring river,
　　　A thousand miles,
　　A single boat among the waves:
　　I dreamed of Hsi-tzu as my companion,
I woke to find dusk's sunlight deflected from village lane.   5
　　　　In how many homes,
　　Behind low walls, hang red almond-blossoms?

From evening clouds could come a bit of rain.
　　　　Going out to pluck flowers—
Who is the girl on the bank?   10
　　　　Ah, what folly!
　　　　Over there,
　　　Willow catkins
Have all been swept by wind into the sky.

                                                         [AL 507]

Where Poem 21 is a parody, Poem 22 is an imitation which reveals Hsin Ch'i-chi's ability to take these conventions seriously. The poem is characterized by the same kind of tenderness and grace associated with the *Hua-chien* style, although the tune pattern used is that of the "long tune," "The Charm of Nien-nu,"[5] which other poets find more suitable for "heroic" poetry (cf. Su Shih's poem written in this meter and quoted in Chapter 3). In the first stanza of Hsin's poem, several motifs familiar to love poetry are included—references to the time as well as to the place; specific details as well as connotative ones—one leading to the other without break. (And, one might note in passing, any one of these motifs is sufficient to occupy a single lyric from the *Hua-chien* collection.) The transition to the second stanza is marked by the two words *wen-tao* (lit., "I have heard it said"), which also serves to increase the esthetic distance; and a further transition occurs in line 16, indicated by one word *liao* ("I imagine"). Thus, what is the most personal statement of the poet is given greater poignancy, since the question is stated only in the last two lines of the poem. For Chinese traditionalist critics, whose criteria of good poetry are "intricateness," or *mi* (lit., "dense" or "thick"), and "tenderness" (*wan*), this poem has the widest appeal. From the point of view of composition, this lyric is characterized by the presence of subtle "veins" or "arteries" (*mai* or *mo*, also meaning "the pulse"), a characteristic also considered a *sine qua non* of lyric poetry by Chinese critics. In other words, through skillful recombination, Hsin has used the commonplaces of the *Hua-chien* style to write a new kind of lyric, employing a tune title least likely to be associated with this kind of poetry.

[POEM 22]

Tune title: The Charm of Nien-nu (*Nien-nu-chiao*)
Title: Written on the Wall [of an inn] at
Tung-liu Village
Date of composition: 1178

The wild-plum has shed all its petals;
Once again the season has scurried by
Past the Ch'ing-ming Festival.
Still, the east wind deludes a traveler's dream
With a night's shiver by the mica screen.   5

Holding a cup in hand by the winding shore,
Or tying my horse to the weeping willow:
So many times have I taken my leave of such a place.
The pavilion is now emptied of its guest:
Only familiar visitors, the swallows, can speak of what
    they knew.   10

I have heard of lovely roads to the east,
Where travelers have watched
From beneath the curtain, maidens' mincing steps.
Old grief, like a spring river, flows on unbroken;
New grief stretches across a thousand clouded peaks.   15
    I imagine that some day
    When we meet again over a flask of wine,
Flowers in the mirror would be hard to pluck;
    Wouldn't you surprise yourself by asking:
"How many hairs are now touched with gray?"   20
                                                            [AL 46–47]

III   Imitation of the Styles of Other Poets
(*T'ao Ch'ien and Li Ch'ing-chao*)

Whether or not it is the sincerest form of flattery, imitation—even
in the most conscious manner—is a commonly accepted practice
among Chinese poets and is never frowned upon (unless, of course,
when the work of someone else is passed off as one's own).[6] This is
understandable especially in view of the richness of the past poetic
tradition. A popular "game" among the literati, for instance, has been
to collect lines from the works of a single poet or of several poets
(most of the time from memory) and, out of a collage of quotations,
to form a new poem. The new poem (which could be either *shih* or
tz'u) is at the same time expected to have a prosodic pattern and
rhyming scheme of its own. This kind of poetry, called *chi-chü* (lit.,
"collected lines"), is of course "written" to display skill or to enter-
tain; and one probably should not expect it to show any originality
of thought or diction. But to readers who can recognize the original
lines, the ingenuity of such an arrangement can be impressive. Poem
23, cited below, is made up of two lines from *Ch'u Tz'u* (in lines
1–2), one line from Su Shih (line 4), and two lines (lines 3 and 5)
from two T'ang poets: Tu Mu (803–852) and Li Ch'iao (644–713).[7]

[POEM 23]

Tune title: Remembering the Prince (*I-wang-sun*)
Title: Saying Farewell [to Someone] at a River
in Autumn. Collecting Lines from Ancient Poetry
Date of Composition: Undetermined

To ascend the mountain, or go down to the river, I see you off;
Of all griefs, no grief is greater than to be parted
  from the living.
There is no need of ascending or going down, to blame
  it all on the setting sun:
  Friends of yesterday are gone;
There are only, year after year, autumn geese flying.   5

[AL 514]

Less common than either the "collecting of lines" or "harmonizing" (*ho*) is the poem of "embellishment," call *yin-kua* in Chinese
(lit., "a bevel" or "beveling"), which is to take a poem from a favorite poet and add words to it, or to delete other words, and, in
general, to rearrange the lines. Hsin Ch'i-chi's admiration for T'ao
Ch'ien is shown in a number of poems; it is, therefore, not surprising
to find that he did more than just allude to T'ao's works or echo his
style. A deliberate attempt at "embellishment" is Poem 24, which
takes lines from a four-word poem in *ku-shih* meter by T'ao Ch'ien,
including its Preface, and rearranges the words into Lyric Meter.
Certainly, the lyric, by itself, cannot be said to be among Hsin's best
efforts; nonetheless, it is a dexterous exercise of craftsmanship, where
success is judged not by considerations of originality but rather by
its technical skill (just as Bach made use of a hymn by Martin
Luther as the *cantus firmus* in his chorale preludes and cantatas).
T'ao Ch'ien's poem "On Stilled Clouds" (*T'ing-yün*),[8] together
with its Preface, is as follows:

Looking at clouds that lie still for a moment in their drifting—evokes
in me a longing for friends. With a flask of new wine, and the garden
burgeoning in its first splendor, I long for friends, but I cannot have my
desire. Sighs and regret fill my heart.

Dark and somber, the stilled clouds!
Misting, drizzling, the seasonal rain!
Everywhere darkness shrouds everything.
All level roads are impassable.

Quietly, I stay in the eastern studio;
The spring wine, I drink alone.
My good friends are far away;
Scratching my head, I wait in vain.

The stilled clouds, dark and somber!
Seasonal rain, mist and drizzle!
Everywhere darkness shrouds everything;
All pathways have become a river.
But I have wine, I have wine!
At leisure, I drink by the eastern window.
I long for my cherished friends,
But no boat or cart allows me to follow my desire.

The trees in my eastern garden,
Their branches and twigs are flourishing again;
In their loveliness they compete
To invite my attention.
Some people say
The days and months march on.
When can we sit together
To tell each other our lives?

Flutter, flutter the flying birds—
Alight on the tall trees in my courtyard.
Preening their feathers, calmly they perch,
Their sweet notes blend.
It is not that I have no other friend,
But I think of you most.
I long for friends, but I cannot have my wish;
What is more unbearable than this regret of mine?

Poem 24 shows the "embellishment" by Hsin.

[POEM 24]
Tune title: Every Sound, *Lentemente* (*Sheng-sheng-man*)
Title: Embellishing Yüan-ming's [T'ao Ch'ien's]'
"Stilled Clouds" Poem
Date of composition: (conj.) 1193–94

The stilled clouds, dark and somber!
Everywhere darkness shrouds everything.
All day long, seasonal rain, mist and drizzle.
Scratching my head, I long for good friends.
In front of my gate, all level pathways have become a river.   5

How clear is the wine! But I drink alone;
    Regret fills my heart,
As I drink, at leisure, by the eastern window, waiting in vain
How I begrudge boats and carts, north and south;
I wish to join them, but where can I follow my desire?   10

I sigh at the stately trees in my eastern garden,
Burgeoning in their first splendor, every twig and leaf,
    To compete once again with the spring wind.
    The days and months march on:
    When can we sit together, undisturbed?   15
Flutter, flutter, coming from I know not where, the flying bird—
    Alight on the tall tree in my courtyard;
    Their sweet talks blend.
    The affairs of those days—
    Let me ask, how many people   20
Have friends who feel like this old man?

[AL 331–32]

Among contemporary and near-contemporary lyricists, Hsin Ch'i-chi appears to have the greatest admiration for the gifted woman poet, Li Ch'ing-chao (Li I-an, 1084–1151),[9] who also came from his native city (Tsinan, Shantung) and, like him, had moved South following the collapse of the Northern Sung dynasty. Although no more than fifty or so of her lyrics (those of indisputable authorship) have survived today, she had wide reputation as a poet and scholar in her own time. The philosopher Chu Hsi spoke of her as "one of the only two literate women of the Dynasty";[10] and a Sung bibliography (Preface dated 1151) listed her collected works of prose and poetry as consisting of twelve *chüan*.[11] Li Ch'ing-chao's extant poems, few as they are, amply demonstrate her skill as a lyricist; her poems are, in the words of one critic, "unmatched" in both "delicacy" and "immediacy."[12] As an artist with words, she is especially admired for her use of the colloquial and vernacular idiom and for her originality of expression.[13] Her achievement must have so impressed Hsin that a number of his lyrics also attempt a colloquial flavor—sometimes with singular success, but most of the time without the spontaneity and grace that mark Li's style. For instance, the line "I long to speak but can't" (*yü-shuo huan-hsiu*), in Poem 32 (included in Chapter 6), comes from a line of Li Ch'ing-chao's: "In how many affairs, I long to speak but can't (*to-shao-shih yü-shuo huan-hsiu*),[14] with the last word *hsiu* meaning "let go," a colloquial expression.

But the four words function most effectively in Hsin's poem; at other times, however, the incorporation of similar phrases does not achieve results as happy as here.

The experimental bent of Hsin's mind is most evident in Poem 25, which bears the title: "Written ... in Imitation of the Style of Li I-an [Li Ch'ing-chao]." That Hsin does not score any spectacular success with his imitation is equally evident if we examine a typical lyric by Li Ch'ing-chao, which contains at least two descriptive details similar to those found in Hsin's poem. Li's lyric is as follows:

To the Tune of "A Prince's Lament" (*Yüan-wang-sun*)[15]
by Li Ch'ing-chao

The wind bestirs a lake to distant ripples:
     It's autumn's dusk.
The red is sparse, the fragrance diminishing;
Only the glimmer of these hills and water is warm to men.
     I cannot count all
     Such infinite charm!

Lotus seeds already formed, lotus leaves are old;
Awash in tinted dew, duckweed flowers and grass by the banks.
Dozing on the sand, sea gulls and terns do not glance back,
     As if they were also chafing
     At your leaving too soon.

In calling his poem an "imitation," Hsin of course must have had in mind what he considered Li's characteristic ways of expression and description, not necessarily any one specific poem. But the heavy use of ejaculatory lines ("such," "what," etc.) and of colloquialisms appears to be among the effects he tries to create in the following poem:

[POEM 25]
     Tune title: Ugly Slave (with Words Added)
          (*Ch'ou-nu-erh chin*)
     Title: Written on the Road to Po-shan, in
          Imitation of the Style of Li I-an
     Date of composition: (conj.) 1182–92

Around a thousand peaks, clouds gather;
A sudden rain, just as quickly over—
Then, distant trees, a setting sun: such scenery!

What a picture!
A wineshop's blue pennant—   5
On the other side of the mountain, there are homes still.
If only one could remain in the glimmer of these hills and water,
    Idling, to live through this one summer!

To awake from noontime stupor,
Pine trees at the window, bamboo at the door—   10
    How very carefree!
Then, when wild birds come flying,
That again is another kind of pleasure.
But I marvel at these white sea gulls,
Seeing people around, want to come down and yet do not come.   15
    My old companions are all here:
Among the newcomers, could there be
Some who wish to speak of something else?

                                             [AL 138–39]

In this poem Hsin uses not only such accepted colloquial expressions in lyric poetry as *tsen-sheng* (line 4; lit., "in what manner"),
but also many other less conventional colloquialisms, such as *i-sha-
erh-chia* (line 2; lit., "a little while in this manner"); *na-pan* (line 6;
"the other side"); *che-i* (line 8; "this one"); *shuo-hua* (line 18; "to
speak"); and so on. The measure word *i-pan* (line 13; lit., "this
kind") has been much admired in the poetry of Li Yü,[16] as well as
in Li Ch'ing-chao. The expression *yü-hsia wei-hsia* (lit., "wish to
come down; not yet come down") reads like an obvious imitation of
Li Ch'ing-chao's two superb lines, which in the original are used to
describe grief: *ts'ai-hsia mei-t'ou; ch'üeh-shang hsin-t'ou.*[17] Literally,
"just about to come down [from] the eyebrow, but [it] climbs up to
the heart"—these lines not only employ the vernacular suffix-word
t'ou for "heart" and "eyebrow" but also make a pun of "climb up"
(*shang*) and "go down" (*hsia*)—making translators despair.[18] But,
applied to sea gulls, and especially in combination with the allusion
of the "alliance" (*meng*, translated as "companions," in line 16),
the colloquial expression has already lost most of its charm. Hsin
might have been undiscriminating in his attempt to combine all these
tag phrases which he associated with Li's style. The failure of this
effort should demonstrate, once for all, that Hsin is not by any
means always a good "imitator."

IV *Literary Allusion and the Poetry of "Bravura"*

It is a common practice among Chinese poets, especially in the writing of *tz'u*, to attempt a kind of grafting, something like a game at "genre-transference," whereby a new lyric is written by incorporating the sentiments (*i*) and the language of traditional poetry (*shih*), or sometimes of another lyric. This exercise in prosodic dexterity is aimed either at capitalizing on the quality of superior lines of poetry, or at bettering the original. In this special use of past literature, Chinese poets reflect a tendency shared by Chinese artists in other media, who often like to display their virtuoso skill by duplicating in one medium the highest achievement possible in another. Witness, for instance, some fine porcelain creations made to resemble not only things in nature, like bamboo, lotus petal, or gourd, but also jade and even bronze vessels. The allusive quality in art is sometimes dictated by convention and sometimes by personal circumstances. Thus, to bemoan one's fate as a second Ch'ü Yüan, or to express aspirations similar to T'ao Ch'ien's, is a simple kind of allusion, present also in Western poetry. (One thinks of Keats's "Of lovely Laura in her light green dress,/ And faithful Petrarch gloriously crowned.") But, to lift words and ideas from a poem by someone else, with the purpose of creating new associations or new meaning, is a kind of bravura exercise which *tz'u* writers most often indulged in.

This kind of game appealed particularly to Hsin Ch'i-chi's erudite mind; and the numerous literary allusions found in his lyrics reveal, not so much his success (which tends to be sporadic), but rather his unerring taste in selecting the best lines from the works of past poets. For example, Tu Fu wrote a justly famous line which reads: "At fourth watch, the mountains disgorge a moon" (*ssu-keng shan t'u yüeh*),[19] the word "watch" referring to one of the five units of the night, with the fifth watch corresponding to daybreak. Here the imagery is conveyed by the word *t'u* (lit., "to spew forth"; "to disgorge"), which describes the suddenness in the moon's coming out of the mountains. Hsin's admiration for this line is reflected in several allusions to it, used in slightly different ways. In one, he takes the last three words and writes: "Mountains disgorge a moon,/ Painted candles are left to be snuffed out by the breeze" [AL 220]; in another lyric, he uses the first two words and the third and fifth words to make up a line of his own which reads: "At the fourth watch, moon on the mountain, the cold creeps upon the mat" (*ssu-keng shan-yüeh han-ch'in-hsi*) [AL 234].

Among the successful efforts, we may cite a line from one poem (to the tune of *Ho-hsin-lang*), where Hsin takes a line from Li Po ("My white hair thirty thousand feet") and adds the two words "hangs down in vain" in the middle.* Or, from another poem (to the tune of *Jui-che-ku*), when he borrows a line from the sixth-century poet Wang Chi (*fl. ca.* 502), which occurs in a couplet[20] as follows:

ch'an	*sao*	*lin*	*yü*	*ching*
cicada	cry noisily	forest	more	quiet

niao	*ming*	*shan*	*keng*	*yu*
bird	cry	mountain	more	dark

The two lines from Hsin ("As the scattered cicadas sound their raspy notes, the woods become more silent;/ In the cold air, the butterflies flutter gently, the chrysanthemums half open") read in the original as follows:

su	*ch'an*	*hsiang*	*se*	*lin*	*yü*	*ching*
scattered	cicada	noise	harsh	forest	more	quiet

leng	*tieh*	*ch'ing*	*fei*	*chü*	*pan*	*kai*
cold	butterfly	lightly	fly	chrysan-themum	half	open

By comparing Hsin's first line with the original, we note the addition of two extra words (besides the change of *sao* to *hsiang*). The two adjectives supplied by Hsin—*su* and *se*—indicate not only the precise quality of the cicadas' cry, which so accentuates the silence of the woods, but also the direction of the noise, its omnipresence. At the same time, he discards what is obviously the more pedestrian of Wang Chi's two lines; where the second half of the original antithetical couplet achieves only the reinforcement of the same effect, Hsin creates his own antithesis, concentrating on visual and sensory details.

---

* Hsin's line reads: *Pai-fa k'ung-ch'ui san-ch'ien-chang*, which except for *k'ung-ch'ui* is identical with Li Po's.

Hsin's less successful attempts at this game often result from his overzealous desire to experiment with the lines of poetry he loved best. For example, in the huge literature of anecdotes about lyric poetry and lyric poets, there is probably no more celebrated story than the one about the poet Feng Yen-ssu's (903–60) supposed encounter with the Second Ruler of the Southern T'ang kingdom, Li Ching (also given as Ying) (916–961), himself a noted *tz'u* writer. Feng is the author of a lyric, descriptive of a woman's longing for her lover, which begins with the following two lines: "The wind suddenly comes up,/ Blows, wrinkles a pond of spring water."[21] Li Ching is the author of another widely praised lyric which contains the following two lines: "In a fine rain, my dream returns to Cock Fort—distant;/ In a small pavilion, the *sheng* [mouth-organ] music is played clear through the cold."[22] (The words for "played clear through" are *ch'ui ch'e*; lit., "blow, penetrate.") According to the story told in *Nan-T'ang shu* by Ma Ling (Preface dated 1105), the ruler of Nan-T'ang, at their meeting, recited Feng's line about the "spring water" and asked, "What has that line to do with you?"[23] And Feng is said to have replied, "That is not as good as Your Majesty's 'In a small pavilion, the *sheng* music is played clear through the cold.'" And His Majesty was greatly pleased by Feng's good taste.

Another lyricist, Yen Chi-tao (*fl.* 1073) is the author of two lines which, because of inversion and the highly concrete imagery, defy smooth translation. The two lines read:

wu	*ti*	*yang*	*liu*	*lou*	*hsin*	*yüeh*
dance	low	poplar	willow	pavilion	heart	moon
	lower					

ko	*chin*	*t'ao*	*hua*	*shan*	*ti*	*feng*[24]
sing	exhaust	peach	flower	fan	bottom	wind

These lines could be paraphrased as: "Danced till the moon sank through the willows seen from the middle ("heart") of the chamber;/ Sang till the breeze gave out from the bottom of the fan with the peach-blossom [design]." In a daring move, Hsin tries to combine Feng's and Yen's lines by writing: "Danced until the moon dropped beyond the flowers;/ Sang clear through the breeze along the willow" (*wu-ti hua-wai yüeh,/ ch'ang-ch'e liu-pien feng*) [AL 469].

This particular combination is decidedly inferior to the two orginial lines, probably because they cannot have been improved upon; but Hsin's ingenuity in "playing with" these lines, which he so obviously admired, is nonetheless remarkable.

V *Diction*

Inventiveness characterizes the diction in Hsin Ch'i-chi's poetry to the same degree. His use of the vernacular idiom, while it never achieved the success of Li Ch'ing-chao, serves him well in those poems written in the jocular vein (see Chapter 6, Poems 29–31). His innovation with diction, however, is not confined to the imitation of one style, or to experimentation with colloquialisms alone. On the one hand, some of his lyrics can be even more vernacular than Li's— as evidenced by such expressions as *chien-hsin-ti* [AL 388] for "attractive or cute" or those vernacular suffix-words like *na* and *mo* [AL 464] or *ti* ("hsiao yin-yin-ti jen lai-ch'ü"[25] [AL 223]. On the other hand, Hsin's erudition often encourages him to use such archaisms borrowed from *Ch'u Tz'u* as *hsieh* or *so* (ancient pronunciation; AL 300) and *hsi*[26] [AL 221, 242, 300, *passim*], or deliberately to compose a song with use of such archaic particles. One such use also involves punning. In a line that reads, "The *hsieh's* of Ch'u have been trimmed into a *luan*" (*Ch'u hsieh ts'ai ch'eng luan*) [AL 404], *luan,* translated sometimes as "envoi," means "the last stanza of a poem" in ancient poetry; it also has the meaning of "disorder." But its earliest meaning, as recorded in *Shuo-wen* (p. 747), is "to manage, or put in order." Punning occurs frequently in Hsin, but it is impossible to reproduce in English. They involve medical terms [AL 144], the names of his concubines, or even his own name (the word *hsin* also means "bitter") [AL 431].

But, it is in between the two extremes or archaism and colloquialism where Hsin scores his greatest successes in experimentation and effects the more dramatic departure from tradition in lyric poetry. I refer here to his frequent use of function words, or particles (*hsü-tzu;* lit., "nonconcrete word," normally restricted to prose). (See Chapter 6 for a fuller discussion.) With the use of such terminal particles, in themselves meaningless words, he creates a type of discursive poetry, hitherto unattempted in the lyric mode. In this style of writing, Hsin remains unchallenged; none among his imitators are able to match him in forcefulness or fluency. (Wherever possible, I have taken into account the force of these particles by using such words in my translation as "indeed" and "how," or interjections like "ah" or "oh"; but there are times when they could just as easily disappear in translation.

In the general area of diction, Hsin frequently shows a preference for concrete words, reflected in the preference of nouns over adjectives, and for the figurative use of verbs, not in their ordinary sense, but connotatively, often suggestive of his tendency toward concretizing the objects he is describing. These two characteristics of his diction are illustrated in the next section, which deals with imagery.

VI *Concrete Imagery*

The first noticeable feature of the vocabulary of Hsin's lyrics is how often the verb is totally omitted. From those poems already cited above, I need refer only to such lines as:

> Outside the gauze window
> Slanting wind, fine rain,
> And a siege of slight chill . . . (from Poem 5)

Or

> Garden after a snow,
> Pavilion by the water's edge,
> Or an ancient assignation in Fairyland. (from Poem 15)

Or

> Seven or eight stars on the far horizon,
> Two or three drops of rain closer by the hill—
> A familiar wineshop by the woods beside the shrine.
>   (from Poem 17)

Then there are other lines where no verb occurs in the original, an absence impossible to preserve in an English translation without risking disastrous pidgin English effect. Two examples are the following lines, where the verbs I have added are enclosed in brackets: "The tune of a *p'i-p'a* [heard] on horseback at the desolate border" (Poem 6, line 9), and "One pine, one bamboo, [is] a real friend;/ Mountain birds, mountain flowers, [are] my brothers" (Poem 12, lines 8–9). There are still other instances where verbs clearly function only as participles, and I have translated them as such; the first three lines of Poem 17 are examples of this type:

> Startled magpies scurrying from the branches in the moonlight,
> The chittering of cicadas in midnight's cool breeze,
> Talk of a bountiful year, in the fragrance of ripening grain.

Let me illustrate this preponderance of concrete imagery in Hsin's lyrics with another poem, followed by an explanation of my method of translation:

[POEM 26]

> Tune title: Pure Serene Music (*Ch'ing-p'ing-yüeh*)
> Title: Impressions on the Road to Po-shan
> Date of composition: (conj.) 1186

> Alongside the willow, the flying bridle:
> Dew-drenched, a traveler's clothes weigh heavily.
> A dozing tern peeks at the sand: the lone shadow moves.
> Should fish and shrimp enter its dream?

> A rivulet, bright moon, scattered stars— 5
> The shadow of a washerwoman, how pretty!
> Smiling, she walks away from the traveler and goes home;
> At the gate, the sound of small children crying.　　　　[AL 138]

Of the eight lines in this poem, only two (the third line of each stanza) contain more than one verb; namely, "peeks" (*k'uei*) and "moves" (*tung*) in line 3 and "smiling" (*hsiao*) and "goes home" (*kuei-ch'ü*; lit., "return-depart") in line 7; the second word in this line, *pei,* could mean "with the back turned" or "turns" or "walks away." In line 4 two verbs occur: the weak verb *yu,* meaning "there is" and *ju,* meaning "to enter," here used *as* a participle. Line 1 (*liu-pien fei-k'ung*; lit., "willow-alongside of fly-bridle") has been translated literally; an alternative reading, by taking *fei* as a verb, could be "a bridle flies by." Line 2 (*lu hsi cheng-i chung*; lit., "dew drench traveler's clothes heavy") contains two words which are normally adjectives: *hsi* (wet) and *chung* (heavy), but here used as verbs; the word *cheng* (from *cheng-fu,* "traveler"), obviously, cannot be considered as a verb since *cheng-i* exists as a compound meaning "traveling clothes." The remaining three lines do not contain a single verb or participle.

VII   *The Imagery of Verbs*

The search for *le mot juste* is a concern shared by all poets whether they write in the traditional style or in the Lyric Meter. But largely, I suppose, because the latter permits a greater latitude in the choice of words, this concern is considered to be of even more crucial importance in lyrics. Ordinary words used in an unusual manner are, as a rule, regarded as a source of concealed, or unexpected, delight; hence, lyricists generally subscribe to the belief that in order for the lines to be "clever" (*ming*), the words must be "quick" (*chieh*).[27] Similar *obiter dicta* abound in the criticism of lyric poetry. The Chinese language, because it permits greater freedom in word order and looser distinctions between parts of speech (than, say, in English), allows the poet to cultivate a vocabulary with richer connotations. In Hsin's poetry, this concern is evident in (1) the subtle differentiation of annotative meanings in the use of ordinary words; (2) inversions of word order; and (3) his predilection for the use of nouns and adjectives as verbs.

Take, for instance, the word *shou*, meaning "to receive, to collect, or to gather." Its literal use may be illustrated by the following line: "Flocks of chickens and ducks: late in the evening, have not yet been *gathered in*" (*shou*) [AL 474]. The same word is used in its figurative sense in another line which I quoted in the last chapter: "Sundered clouds, coursing above the river, are *gathered up* [*shou*] at dusk" [AL 153]. In still another line, in a poem cited in Chapter 4, the same word is used to mean "to gather in and to be put away, not for use for some time," in the line "Unwilling still to *store away* [*shou*] the lingering cold." Similar figurative use of common verbs can be found in many poems—most noticeably in connection with such words as *jan* (to dye) and *hsün* (to fumigate) [AL 463]; *jang* (to make wine or to brew) [AL 210]; *chien* (lit., "to cut") and *ts'ai* (to cut out a pattern, as in dress-making, or to trim), all of which are among Hsin's favorite words. "A line of my verse is trimmed [*chien*] and shaped [*ts'ai*] by the spring breeze" (Poem 18, line 1) may be compared with the following literal use of *chien-p'o* (lit., "to cut and to break") in "A lone goose rises . . ./ *Cuts and cleaves* the water of Pine River" [AL 510].

VIII   *Word Order and Inversion*

The pattern of subject-verb-object (S-V-O) is the normal pattern in Chinese as it is in English, and the inversion, of course, has its

desired effect. Hsin uses both patterns effectively. First, examples
of the normal pattern:

hung-lien	*hsiang-i*	*hun*	*ju*	*tsui*
red-lotus	each other-lean	completely	look-like	drunk

pai-niao	*wu-yen*	*ting*	*tzu*	*ch'ou*
white-bird	no-speech	must	self	grieve
				[AL 152]

(Red lotus flowers, leaning each upon each, appear as if drunk;
The white birds, all silent, must be communing with their private grief.)

fu	*t'ien*	*shui*	*sung*	*wu-ch'iung*	*shu*
float	sky	water	send-off	limitless	tree

tai	*yü*	*yün*	*mai*	*i-pan*	*shan*
bring-with	rain	cloud	bury	half	mountain
					[AL 185]

(Floating in the sky, the river bids farewell to numberless trees;
Accompanied by the rain, the clouds have buried half a mountain.)

Inversions of the S-V-O patern are many, the simplest type of which
may be seen in the following couplet (where the normal order in
the first line would be *ming-yüeh ta kuei lu*):

kuei	*lu*	*ta*	*ming*	*yüeh*
return-home	road	tread	bright	moon

jen	*ying*	*kung*	*p'ai*	*hui*
man	shadow	to share;	pace-to-and-fro	
		together		[AL 110]

(Under a bright moon, I tread the road home;
And I pace to and fro with only my shadow accompanying me.)

At other times, especially in lines that require parallelism, in either
successive or alternate lines, the inversion helps to place the emphasis
upon the object. A good example is the following lines from the

poem (to the tune of *Ch'in-yüan-ch'un*), entitled "On the Eve of the Completion of My New Villa on Ribbon Lake" [AL 76]:

> Who promised himself hills and clouds—
>   All his life's ambition.
> Caps and gowns he mocked
> As lighter than dust.

In the original, these lines read as follows:

shen	*yün*	*shan*	*tzu*	*hsü*
why	cloud	mountain	self	promise

	p'ing -	*sheng*	*i -*	*ch'i*
	all -	life	mind, ambition	

	i	*kuan*	*jen*	*hsiao*
	cap	gown	man (I)	laugh at
				(mock)

	ti -	*shih*	*ch'eng -*	*ai*
	all is		dust particles	

Here the two phrases "clouds and mountains" and "caps and gowns" (occurring as a metonymy for "titles of office") are placed before the verbs "to promise" and "to mock," respectively. Another case of even greater ambiguity due to inversion may be illustrated by the following lines:

chou	*yung*	*nuan*	*fang*	*hung*	*hsing*	*yü*
day	long,	warm,	tumble	red	apricot	rain
or daylight	forever	warmth				

feng	*ch'ing*	*fu*	*ch'i*	*ch'ui*	*yang*	*li*
wind	sunny-day	lift	up	hanging	willow	strength
						[AL 64]

These could be paraphrased as:

> All day long, in the warmth of the sun,
>   red apricot-blossoms are blown down, helter-skelter, like rain;
> On a sunny day, the hanging willows are supported by the breeze.

Another version might be:

> All day long, the warmth of the sun causes
> the red apricot-blossoms to tumble down like rain;
> On a sunny day, the breeze lends all its strength
> to lift up the branches of the hanging willows.

Occasionally, a parallel couplet will involve inversion in one of the lines, but none in the other, as in the following:

ku	*ho*	*nan*	*shui*	*ya*
withered	lotus	difficult	sleep	duck

su	*yü*	*ang*	*t'ien*	*t'ang*
sparse	rain	furtively	add-to	creek

[AL 469]

> (Ducks doze uneasily among withered lotus;
> Light rain in darkness fills the pond.)

Both regular inversion (in the first four words of each line) and intentional imbalance are found in the following couplet [AL 162]:

ou	*hua*	*yü*	*hsi*	*ch'ien*	*hu*	*yeh*
lotus	flower	rain	wet	former	lake	night

kuei	*chih*	*feng*	*tan*	*hsiao*	*shan*	*shih*
laurel	branch	wind	calm	small	hill	time

which may be translated as:

> Lotus-flowers wet with rain—the lake of yesternight;
> Laurel branches calm in the wind—that moment on a small hill.

IX   *The Use of Adjectives and Nouns as Verbs*

Given the freedom from rigid rules governing grammatical distinctions, Chinese poets are able to cultivate the use of words in a transferred part of speech rather than in their usual order. And many lines of poetry have become justifiably famous because of such liberties. A celebrated instance is the memorable line of Wang An-shih's (1021–86): "Spring wind has by itself turned green the bank south

of the River" (*ch'un-feng tzu-lü chiang-nan an*),[28] where the word
for "green," or *lü*, is used as a verb (cf. Hardy's "All smalling slowly
to the gray sea-line"[29]). Hsin's adeptness in this respect may be
illustrated by line 16 of Poem 6: "On the bank of the mournful *I*
River the west wind *chills*," the original of which reads: *I-shui hsiao-
hsiao hsi-feng leng*, with the last word *leng* meaning "cold" or
"chilly." To cite one more example, a line from a poem on plum-
blossoms reads:

hsüeh	*yen*	*ping*	*hun*
snow	gorgeous, beautiful	ice	soul, spirit

[AL 435]

This may be rendered as: "Made wanton by the snow, the spirit of
ice." It should be pointed out that "spirit of ice" is a conventional
epithet for plum-blossoms; but the adjective *yen* is most commonly
used to describe the fleshly beauty of a woman; it connotes all kinds
of sensuous appeal, the very opposite of the ethereal quality of the
flower he describes. Used as a transitive verb—a remarkable feat in
itself—the word fulfills the double juxtaposition of body with soul,
and contrasts the gorgeous but ephemeral quality of spring with the
aloofness and loneliness of spiritual beauty.

Nouns are also used as verbs, although less frequently than adjectives. A more conventional example is the use of *han*, meaning
"cold," as "a cold place" in line 7 of Poem 36, included in the next
chapter. A more interesting instance is found in the following lines,
also about plum-blossoms:

Eternally chaste and fair, how could she deign to pander herself?
She only needs some lines of verse to arrange this affair!

[AL 498]

The word which I have translated as "pander" is *mei*, meaning "a
matchmaker." It is rarely used as a verb, although *Shuo-wen*, the
earliest Chinese dictionary, defines this word as a verb, in the sense
of *mo*, or "to arrange a marriage between two families."[30] Equally
clever, although it "borrows" from the work of a T'ang poet, is the
use as a verb of the word *shih*, *meaning* "a louse," in line 9 of Poem
36 (but not in the same sense as "louse up" in American slang).
Shih, a variety of blood-sucking insect like a bedbug, is common
and widely detested in China; its earliest occurrence in literature is

in a philosophical work of the Warring States period, in the sense of "parasites" or "evils of society." A T'ang poet, Han Yü, used this word in a poem about harsh officials, to mean "to prey upon the people,"[31] as one would say today "like a leech." In Poem 36, however, Hsin borrows this word to refer to himself, in a self-deprecating manner, as one would say today "like a flea," since he is describing an imaginary meeting with two famous Chinese poets, Li Po and Su Shih. This line I have translated as "I, the unworthy one, also among them" (*wo i shih ch'i-chien*).

It is the same heightened use of language in English dramatic poetry which makes characters as different as Iago and Cleopatra into such nonpareil poetical characters; compare, for instance, Iago's "To *lip* a wanton in a secure couch and to suppose her chaste" (*Othello,* IV. i. 72) and Cleopatra's "A hand that kings/ Have *lipp'd* and trembled kissing" (*Antony and Cleopatra,* II. v. 29–30). Or, compare the Chinese lyric poet's whimsical use of *shih* with Coriolanus' "Though in Rome *litter'd*—not Romans—as they are not,/ Though *calv'd* i' the porch o' the Capital" (*Coriolanus,* III. i. 238–39) and Antony's "The hearts/ That *spaniel'd* me at heels, to whom I gave/ Their wishes, do discandy, melt their sweets/ On blossoming Caesar" (*Antony and Cleopatra,* IV. xii. 20–23).

X *Summing Up*

To conclude this discussion of Hsin's imagery and diction, I cite a poem [Poem 27] in which colloquialism is combined with striking metaphors, and seriousness with whimsicality.

[POEM 27]

Tune title: Song of the South (*Nan-ko-tzu*)
Title: In the Mountains, Sitting Up at Night
Date of composition: Undetermined

Worldly concerns are depleted from the beginning;
The heart in autumn is clear to its very depth.
Deep night still hears words exchanged by the pillow:
Let me ask: what affairs from the bottom of the clear stream
    Have not yet been smoothed over?   5

The moon appears brighter to those nearer to grief;
A cock's crow is heard at the farthest point.
In these things there is neither profit nor fame:

Then why beyond the hills, before daybreak,
Are travelers taking the road?   10
[AL 502–3]

The first two lines of each stanza in this poem are, respectively,
as follows:

shih	*shih*	*ts'ung*	*t'ou*	*chien*
world,	affair,	from	head,	subtract
life	event		start	

ch'iu	*huai*	*ch'e*	*ti*	*ch'ing*
autumn	heart	clear-	bottom	pure
		through		(11. 1–2)

yüeh	*tao*	*ch'ou*	*pien*	*pai*
moon	reaching,	grief	edge	white
	upon arrival at			

chi	*hsien*	*yüan*	*ch'u*	*ming*
cock	before,	distant	place	cry or
	first			crow (11: 6–7)

The use of *chien*, meaning "to subtract from a total sum," or "to
lessen," is remarkable for economy in describing how life is "drained,"
"diminished bit by bit," or "depleted"; and it is paralleled by *ch'ing*,
an adjective functioning as a verb to mean "stays pure." There is
clever "matching" in *t'ou* (head) and *ti* (bottom); and *ts'ung-t'ou*
is a colloquial expression, as are several other words in the rest of
the poem. For "exchange" (line 3) the original uses the verb *sung*
meaning "to send back and forth." Lines 6–7 could be translated
more literally as:

The moon whitens on the edge of grief;
A cock crows first at a distant place.

The use of *pai* to mean "whiten" is not uncommon in Chinese poetry;
but the colloquial usage of *tao*, functioning adverbially (the same as
in the colloquial speech today), lends slight ambiguity to the line.
Paraphrased loosely, it means: "The moon does not turn white until
it reaches the edge of grief." The word *pien* (side or edge) also requires explanation: it indicates "nearness" to a place, not the place
itself. Since the phrase "not ... until," implied in the usage of *tao*,

suggests a comparison, as does the adverb "first" in the next line, the use of comparatives in the translation is, I think, justifiable for both lines.

In other words, the first of the two lines says: The moon appears most nearly white to people who are getting nearer to grief (as if moving there to take up their residence). Or, Beauty is appreciated most by those who live in close proximity to sorrow. The second line, perhaps just as cryptic if left in the original word order, is not as hard to paraphrase. Whether or not it can be proven that the first note of the cock's crowing, even admitting the stillness of dawn, can be first heard at the farthest point, this line could have been intended to describe the homesickness of a traveler. Someone who is eager to resume his journey in the early hours of the day, or who may have been kept awake the previous night, is likely to be the first person to "catch" the first sound of cock's crowing. The mention of a nocturnal interior scene in line 3 (which literally reads, "Night deep, still send pillowside sound"), to be contrasted with the morning activity of the next day, is, of course, an exercise in humor. The first of the two stanzas ends with a frivolous question, and the second ends with a serious one.

Nurtured on the best poetic traditions of the past, Hsin Ch'i-chi set out to demonstrate that lyric poetry was able to accommodate all styles, including the contemporary idiom of his day. He was as much at home with the language of the ancient anthology, *Ch'u Tz'u,* as he was with all the motifs of the "newer" poetry of romantic love, as found in the *Hua-chien* collection—and no two anthologies could be as unlike each other as these two. While Hsin's erudition has never failed to win the just admiration of traditionalist Chinese critics, it is the inventiveness in his use of language that has all too often been ignored. More than an inheritor of past literary conventions, he labored with devotion and skill at their enrichment; he adapted the craft of *tz'u* composition to his personal needs and to newer demands, including those of philosophic speculation (discussed in the next chapter) undreamed of by the originators of "song-poems." As we have seen, his use of tradition is neither blind nor timid; and it seldom fails to show what T. S. Eliot calls "a perception . . . not only of the pastness of the past, but of its presence,"[32] or a poet's ability to feel that "the whole of the literature of [one's] own country has a simultaneous existence and composes a simultaneous order."[33] Hsin Ch'i-chi would have readily agreed with Eliot's observation that "The dead writers are . . . [p]recisely . . . that which we know."[34]

CHAPTER 6

The Poetry of Paradox
Wit and Allusion

> There should be no flight from
> irony and paradox in writing
> poetry, rather an insistence on
> them. They are often the source, I
> think, of what richness and honesty
> we sense in a poem.
>   —Richard Wilbur,
>   "The Genie in the Bottle"*

> Poetry is to be diagnosed as
> "dangerous" because it evokes and
> recalls, is a kind of *anamnesis* of,
> i.e. is an effective recalling of,
> something loved.
>   —David Jones,
>   *The Anathémata*†

In "The Language of Paradox," Cleanth Brooks has said that even though Wordsworth's sonnet "Composed upon Westminster Bridge, September 3, 1802" contains "very flat writing and some well-known comparisons," the lyric somehow expresses a "sense of awed surprise"[1] because of the presence of irony. The "beauty of the morning" which the City "doth wear" heightens the feeling of how the city was actually alive when the sun "did ... more beautifully steep ... valley, rock or hill." Like Wordsworth's sonnet, Hsin Ch'i-chi's lyric cited at the end of the last chapter contains some well-

---

* *The Gist of Poetics,* ed. Clyde E. Henson (New York: Twayne, 1964), p. 107.

† *The Anathémata* (London, 1952; New York: The Viking Press, 1965), p. 21.

worn comparisons and also some redeeming features. In a different way, the Chinese poet describes in that poem the vanity of man's toil and sacrifices from the viewpoint of the Taoist philosophy of *wu-wei*. In this chapter, I shall examine a number of Hsin's witty and allusive poems, the product of an erudite mind steeped in the philosophy of Lao Tzu and Chuang Tzu.

I *Poetry of Paradox*

In discussing paradox in Chinese poetry, one must distinguish between the verbal paradox and the more complex paradox of meaning. Even on the verbal level, one must mention, and quickly dismiss as only a kind of superficial paradox, what looks like an English oxymoron ("faith unfaithful," "living death," *etc.*), but which is, in Chinese, not a special figure of speech, but an inherent feature of the language. I refer to such antithetical compounds, which abound even in everyday vocabulary, that denote single concepts (e.g., *ta-hsiao*, lit., "large-small," meaning "size" or *to-shao*, lit., "much-little," meaning "quantity"). Of course, the use of pairs of contrasting terms later became a prominent feature in Chinese poetry when required to meet the demands of antithesis in successive lines of verse. But even before the vogue of the "regulated verse," when T'ao Ch'ien wrote, in "A Song of Condolence"[2] (in James R Hightower's translation[3]) three of the four lines contain antithetical compounds:

> He no longer knows success or failure.
> What has he to do with right and wrong?
> After a thousand or ten thousand years
> Who will know his fame or disgrace? [3]

Phrases like "sink and float" (*ch'en-fu*, from line 18 of Poem 35) and "the eclipse and the perfection" (*k'uei-ch'üan*, from line 17 of Poem 36) are examples of these compounds which seem paradoxical but actually are not.

Perhaps less familiar to Western readers is the paradox on the level of meaning (sometimes combined with verbal paradox). A good instance of this kind of paradox in lyric poetry is the three lines from Li Yü (in James J. Y. Liu's translation)[4]:

Chien pu tuan	Cut it, yet unbroken,
Li huan luan	Arrange it, yet entangled:
Shih li ch'ou	Such is the sorrow of separation?

Thus, when Hsin Ch'i-chi writes, "Smallest stirrings of the infinite" (Poem 38, line 5), even when it is an allusion, or "all emptiness is contained in infinitude" (Poem 37, line 6), which is his own line— he is using paradox in much the same manner as the Metaphysical poets. One thinks of such lines as Donne's "Take me to you, imprison me, for I,/ Except you'enthrall me, never shall be free,/ Nor ever chaste, except you ravish me" (*Holy Sonnets,* XIV). In Chinese, as in English, the language of poetry is never far removed from the language of paradox, although the frame of reference might be slightly different.

The use of paradox, either in its rhetorical guise (as in oxymoron), or when it involves the very core of meaning, is as familiar in Chinese poetry as in Western. It is in the area of the philosophy of paradox—Taoism—where the Westerner may encounter a notion that is not entirely familiar. Western philosophies, especially systematic Western philosophies, tend to be either dualistic (Platonism, Manichaeanism), or dialectical (Hegelianism), but they are seldom, at base at least, paradoxical. Even in Christianity, when one encounters paradox, it is merely used to illustrate some other teaching. "But many that are first shall be last; and last shall be first" is paradoxical only in form, but not in content: it teaches a nonparadoxical moral of justice. But the essence of Taoism cannot but be expressed in paradoxes.

From the eighty-one chapters of the earliest Taoist classic, the *Tao-te-ching* (which is, in part, rhymed), one reads such lines as these (in John C. H. Wu's translation):

> Bend and you will be whole.
> Curl and you will be straight.
> Keep empty and you will be filled.
> Grow old and you will be renewed. . . .[5] (Chapter 22)

> The softest of all things
> Overrides the hardest of all things.[6] (Chapter 43)

Or, take a typical passage from the writings of Chuang Tzu, or Chuang Chou, a philosopher of the fourth century B.C. (the book-itself, simply known as the *Chuang-tzu,* consists of thirty-three chapters, or sections, believed to have "circulated in something like their present form from the second century B.C.")[7]:

There is nothing in the world bigger than the tip of an autumn hair, and Mount T'ai [the highest mountain known in ancient China] is tiny. No one has lived longer than a dead child, and P'eng-tsu died young. Heaven and earth were born at the same time I was, and the ten thousand things are one with me.[8] (translation by Burton Watson)

Paradox lies at the very truth of Taoism.

It should be obvious from the preceding discussion how fond Hsin Ch'i-chi is of allusions. Hsin's familiarity with the *Chuang-tzu* is borne out in poem after poem. For our purpose, we may note that while the number of allusions made by the poet to this book alone is staggering,[9] Hsin's use of the *Chuang-tzu* is unlike his use of any other book, including the *Shih chi* (*Records of the Grand Historian*), in thoroughness and pervasiveness. Of the thirty-three chapters, Hsin makes allusions to twenty-five of them. While the composite or allusive use of the *Chuang-tzu* will be discussed later in the chapter, I should like to illustrate here what may be termed an "imbedded paradox," which is essentially an expression of the Taoist mind, accountable for many of Hsin Ch'i-chi's finest lines.

To be sure, Hsin Ch'i-chi is not the first Chinese poet to write in this style of poetry: a pre-eminent exponent of the use of paradox in poetry is T'ao Ch'ien. Take, for instance, his "Drinking Wine" Poem Number 5, which reads, in a translation by James R. Hightower,[10] as follows:

> I built my hut [*lu*] beside a traveled road [*jen-ching*]
> Yet hear no noise [*hsüan*] of passing carts and horses.
> You would like to know how it is done?
> With the mind [*hsin*] detached [*yüan*], one's place [*ti*]
>   becomes remote [*p'ien*].
> Picking chrysanthemums by the eastern hedge
> I catch sight of the distant [*yao-jan*] southern hills. . . .

Here, several far-reaching paradoxes can be observed, all of which are "imbedded" in the imagery by means of implied comparisons. A hut, or an ordinary dwelling place (*lu*), is normally found in an "inhabited area" (of men), or *jen-ching*, not "in the wilds" (which is the meaning of *p'ien*); it is, therefore, subject to all kinds of noises (*hsüan*), as of carts and horses. A man's mind (*hsin*; lit., "heart"), when it is not freed from desires and passions (its "noises"), is like a hut located at a busy crossroad. And only when the mind, or heart, makes itself "distant" (*yüan*) from things, can it become like a place (*ti*, lit. also meaning "earth") situated in the wilds. Then, and only then, the distant southern mountains can be seen, from afar (*yao-jan*), from the eastern hedge. In other words, to a mind (or heart) practiced in the Taoist concept of quietism, the distant can be near, and all noise hushed.

A lyric of Hsin's written in much the same style is Poem 12, from which I quote the first stanza:

> I did not take the road to the Capital:
> Instead, I made mountain monasteries tired of greeting me.
> Where lay the unflavored, among flavors, I sought my joy;
> Midway between the useful and the useless, I passed my life.

A paraphrase of the first two lines might be: "I do not travel [*hsing*] the road that leads to Ch'ang-an,/ But I make mountain monasteries tired of meeting and welcoming me." In the last two lines, the poet amplifies these two contrasted situations. Where other people show a taste for the "flavored" (*wei*) things, he "seeks" (*ch'iu*) his happiness among "the unflavored" (*wu-wei*); where other people may be known for their "talents" (*ts'ai*) or considered as "untalented" (*pu-ts'ai*), he "passes" (*kuo*) his life, or spends his days, somewhere in between. In other words, the poet implies, only the "unflavored things" in life can bring happiness; and the only place safe enough for one to spend his life is to be counted neither among the untalented nor among the prominent. Both of these statements (as pointed out in the Notes) are, respectively, derived from the *Tao-te-ching* and the *Chuang-tzu*; but Hsin Ch'i-chi makes use of them in his poetry to illustrate his personal situation and his own feelings. In so doing, he has turned these two paradoxes of philosophy into the poetry of paradox.

II   *An Autobiographical Poem: Hsin's Elegy on the Death of Chu Hsi*

The pervasive influence of the philosophy of Lao Tzu and Chuang Tzu upon Hsin Ch'i-chi's works can be further attested to by Poem 28—a lyric which, with respect to the circumstances of its composition at least, is a bit ironical even if the paradoxical nature of its content has been mitigated by the sadness and solemnity of the occasion. This poem bears the title of "While Reading the *Chuang-tzu*, I Heard of the Passing of Chu Hui-an [courtesy-name of Chu Hsi],"[11] although the reference to Chu Hsi is deleted from the title of the poem as it appears in the earlier four-*chüan* edition, which reads only as "Thoughts upon Reading the *Chuang-tzu*."[12] Since the text of the poem in the earlier edition also offers other discrepancies—a major variant being the omission[13] of the word "posthumous" (*i*) in line 12,—and there are a few other internal evidences (which I shall enumerate in the Notes), I believe this poem to be, in fact, an elegy written on the death of his friend, the Neo-Confucian philosopher, Chu Hsi. Chu's philosophy being under the court's ban at the time of the printing of the earlier edition, it is entirely possible that not only the title of the poem was changed, but the word "posthumous" was left out to make the poem read less like an elegiac piece than it was. The poem is as follows:

[POEM 28]

> Tune title: Grateful for Imperial Favor (*Kan-huang-en*)
> Title: While Reading the *Chuang-tzu*, I Heard of the
> Passing of Chu Hui-an [Chu Hsi]
> Date of composition: (conj.) 1200

On my desk are several books,
    Which, if not *Chuang*, would be *Lao*.
He who can say: "Forget the words" begins to know;
    Yet ten thousand words, thousands of lines:
    He himself cannot forget—how laughable!   5
This morning, the season of rain has just ended;
    The blue sky how lovely.

One low valley, one small hill;
    A light jacket, and a short hat—
The times when my white hairs multiply, old friends become fewer. 10
    Tzu-yün is now gone from us;
Might he have left some posthumous drafts of a Mystic Book?
    The river flows on, day and night:
    When will it ever end?

[AL 382]

In this "In Memoriam" poem, Hsin Ch'i-chi pays a high tribute to his friend by comparing him to Yang Hsiung (whose courtesy-name was Tzu-yün, 53 B.C.–A.D. 18), one of the most eminent Confucian scholars of Han times. The reference to Lao Tzu and Chuang Tzu in the opening lines could be simply a statement of the actual situation. Perhaps the poet found it just a little ironical that he should have received the news of his friend's death while he was reading his favorite Taoist philosophers. As Chu Hsi was such a prolific writer and commentator of Confucian classics, Hsin could easily be led to contemplate upon the wisdom of Chuang Tzu's remark: "Words exist because of meaning; once you've gotten the meaning, you can forget the words [wan-yen]."[14] It is evident from this episode that neither his admiration for his friend nor the grief of a personal loss could deprive Hsin of his faculty to consider the paradox of the situation. Paradox, "the source of richness and honesty" in poetry, lies at the heart of his thinking.

III   *Poetry of Wit*

Irony, a paradox of situation, can be seen in many of Hsin Ch'i-chi's lyrics. Usually accompanied by word-play, it is often directed either at the foolishness of intellectual pretension (Poems 29 and 30) or at the most trivial things in life (Poem 31). Or, it may embody, as in Poems 32–34, his most serious thought, expressed in his inimitable manner to point out the incongruity between expectation and reality. Poem 29, cited below, makes use of one literary allusion to elucidate, in a humorous manner, a well-known Taoist paradox that it is the soft which overcomes the strong; while Poem 30, with a reference to T'ao Ch'ien, expresses with gentle irony the contrast between the Buddhist way of life, and its emphasis on the extinction of all desires, with the Taoist view that self-denial is not the only road to happiness (or health).

[POEM 29]

Tune title: Divination Song (*Pu-suan-tzu*)

Title: My Teeth Have Fallen Out

Date of composition: Undetermined

What is hard is never firm or strong;
What is soft is hard to be dislodged or destroyed.
If you don't believe, open your mouth and look:
The tongue still there, but the teeth are gone.

Already hollow are the two side-chambers;   5
Now the middle is open wide.
Let me tell this to my children, and please don't laugh at the Old Man:
"Like the dog's kennel, it's for you to walk through."

[AL 206]

[POEM 30]

Tune title: Divination Song (*Pu-suan-tzu*)
Title: Sick from Drinking
Date of composition: (conj.) 1196

One left and sought to be an Immortal;
The other left and sought to be a Buddha;
The Immortal, after a thousand cups, got sodden-drunk;
But his skin and bone were like metal and stone.

If abstinence could lead to health,   5
Buddha would have lived a hundred eons;
But at eighty and some odd years, he entered Nirvana:
Then let me partake of this thing within the cup.

[AL 302–3]

The next two poems satirize, on a more mundane level, the man-and-wife (or concubine) relationship, occasioned by specific incidents in Hsin's life. These light lyrics of fancy and humor are written in a highly colloquial language, and they also poke fun at the themes of the *Hua-chien* style of poetry.

One should keep in mind that in the traditional society of China the question of monogamy versus polygamy did not exist, and the social system permitted a man's having one or more concubines, who usually occupied a more subservient position in the family than the wife. At one time or another, Hsin must have enjoyed the companionship of five or six concubines,[15] about whom he wrote several lyrics. According to a story (found in a contemporary account published in 1194),[16] which is most probably true, Hsin once "presented" one of his concubines called Cheng-cheng (the word also means "neat" or "round") to a doctor who had cured his wife of an illness, as the agreed-upon payment. The first stanza of the lyric reads:

The doctor asked for his fee;
Where could I find that much money?
There is still one Cheng-cheng
Who could fill up a gift-box or tray.

[AL 191]

In another lyric, a *shih-che* ("waiting-maid") named Fei-ch'ing is mentioned in the title as the poet's amanuensis in copying the text of that poem (AL 195; title found only in the four-*chüan* edition). In another lyric, "Inscription on the Portrait of Ah-ch'ing" ("Ah" being a common prefix of familiarity found in names), Hsin described the girl's charm and praised her singing, dancing ability, ending with these lines: "Sometimes, while drunk, I would call for Ch'ing-ch'ing,/ And people would laugh and ask who it was" (AL 487–88). If these three names (Fei-ch'ing, Ah-ch'ing, and Ch'ing-ch'ing) refer to the same person, Fen-ch'ing of Poem 31 must have been indeed a talented lady.

[POEM 31]
    Tune title: Immortal at the Magpie Bridge (*Ch'üeh-ch'iao-hsien*)
        Title: Seeing [Concubine] Fen-ch'ing Off
        Date of composition: Undetermined

    Sedan-chair now ready,
    Chattels set to go;
    The cuckoo's one note: "Hurry."
From now on, every step a backward glance:
But how could that last out a thousand miles and more?   5

    The place where you once walked,
    The place where you once sang—
    In vain, the fragrance falls from the swallows' nest.
Don't suspect the white-haired one has no feeling:
There will be times when he will miss you.   10
                                  [AL 485]

The next group of poems contains three of Hsin Ch'i-chi's best-known lyrics, with Poem 32 being probably his most translated poem (at least nine versions in English; cf. Finding List of Titles and Translations). In theme and style, they are the quintessence of a philosopher-artist's mind. Poem 32, for instance, can be described simply as a poetic version of the *non sequitur* replies of Chuang Tzu;[17] and Poem 33 is an example of a "pseudological debate." But what is evident throughout is the poet's imaginative use of the resources of the language, whatever the source and theme. These poems reveal how the common objects of the phenomenal world and ordinary human experience can be shaped, with resourcefulness, into the language of poetry.

Simple repetition, the use of the same word in a line, is most adroitly employed in Poem 34, in the last line of each stanza. These lines read in the original: *i-tsui i-yu i-shui* [internal rhyme],/ *kuan-*

chu kuan-shan kuan-shui. The word *i* means "it is proper or suitable to do something," followed by verbs; and the word *kuan* means "to be in charge of something," or "to be concerned with," followed by nouns. Even more remarkable is the control exhibited in the repetition of an entire line, as in Poem 32, where this device marks a far cry from, for example, the simple repeated refrains in the *Shih ching* (*Book of Poetry*). Here, the tune pattern requires that the first of the two internal lines in each stanza syntactically complete the thought of the previous line and that the second of the repeated lines lead to the line that follows. (The insistence upon *enjambment,* so important to the structure of this tune pattern, has been ignored by most English translations I have seen.) The Chinese form, though not as complex as the eight-line, two-rhyme triolet of medieval French poetry, achieves the tone of light banter in about the same way as, say, Henry Austin Dobson's "Rose-Leaves."[18]

[POEM 32]
Tune title: Ugly Slave (*Ch'ou-nu-erh*)
Title: Written on the Wall [of an Inn] on the
Road to Po-shan [Monastery]
Date of composition: (conj.) 1188

While I was young, I did not know sorrow's taste:
    I loved to climb many-storied towers.
    I loved to climb many-storied towers—
To write new rhymes and force myself to speak of grief.

But now that I have known all of sorrow's taste,   5
    I long to speak but can't.
    I long to speak but can't—
Except to say, "What a cool autumn day!"

                                      [AL 137]

[POEM 33]
Tune title: West River Moon (*Hsi-chiang-yüeh*)
Title: Random Thoughts
Date of composition: Undetermined

While drunk, I knew only to laugh and make merry;
    Where's the time to grieve?
Lately, I've come to know ancient tomes,
    To believe in them was all wrong.

Last night I lay drunk by the pine tree,   5
And I asked the pine, "How drunk am I?"
Half fearing the pine was moving to lift me up,
With one hand pushing the pine, I said, "Go away."

                                              [AL 486–87]

[POEM 34]
                Tune title: West River Moon (*Hsi-chiang-yüeh*)
            Title: Bidding My Children to Attend to Family Affairs
                    Date of composition: Undetermined

Myriad affairs, like mist or cloud, as swiftly pass;
With age, the rushes and willows sear.
And now what business fits me best?
Fit to get drunk, fit to roam, fit to sleep!

Better hurry to pay your tax and levies,   5
Balance accounts and expenditure.
Your Old Sire still tends to some things—
Tends the bamboo, tends the hills, tends the lake!

                                              [AL 432–33]

Some of Hsin Ch'i-chi's poetry might be labeled as poems of cosmic
humor. A cardinal belief of philosophical Taoism, the freedom of
man's mind, is celebrated not only in the teachings of Chuang Tzu
but also in the style of his writing. Passage upon passage, literally,
soar with the imagination of its author which embraces the entire
universe: from the flight of the great bird called a roc flying ninety
thousand miles straight into the sky down to ants and millepedes. Or,
with the deliberateness of a modern scientist in the laboratory but
without the latter's tools of research, he would intuitively ask such
questions as whether the minnows know themselves to be happy in
the water or whether butterflies could dream themselves to be philosophers. A number of Hsin Ch'i-chi's lyrics reflect the same kind of
paradoxical whimsicality, asking imponderable questions of univeral
import, and cavorting easily among the heavens.

    The earliest manifestion of this poetic style in Chinese literature
is found in the "Heavenly Questions" poem (referred to in the title
of Poem 35) of *Ch'u Tz'u*. This poem from the ancient anthology,
however, merely consists of a series of short passages, more in the
nature of riddles, such as: "How does Heaven co-ordinate its mo-
tions? Where are the twelve Heavenly Houses divided? How are the

sun and moon connected with them, and the stars spaced out over them? . . . Who built the ten-storied tower of jade?"[19] (translation by David Hawkes). And the motif of a dream-journey, although managed in a more sustained and serious manner, is also the most distinguishing feature of *Li Sao*, from the same anthology, as seen in such lines as:

> I watered my dragon steeds at the Pool of Heaven,
> And tied the reins up to the Fu-sang tree.
> I broke a sprig of the Jo-tree to strike the sun with . . .
> The Bird of Heaven gave notice of my comings.[20]

But it is only in the poetry of Li Po and Su Shih when the use of cosmic imagery for whimsical effect appears more frequently and as a device to allow for a poet's more direct expression of individual feelings. Witness Li Po's many poems written about the moon; one of these poems, "Drinking Alone Under the Moon," for instance, contains the following celebrated lines:

> I lift my cup to invite the bright moon,
> To join me and my shadow and make a group of three. . . .
> Forever, let us plight a friendship without human ties;
> And await each other at the Milky Way in the distance.[21]

Or, the apostrophe to the moon, from Su Shih's equally famous lyric:

> When will there be another bright moon?
> Holding a jug of wine, I ask the blue sky.
> In the celestial palace, I wonder,
> What time of the year is this night?
> I yearn to waft there with the wind,
> But fear that in the jasper tower under jade canopies
> It would be so cold as to be insufferable.
> So I rise to dance and frolic with my shadow:
> No place is better than to be here among men.[22]

In the second stanza of this lyric, Su goes on to describe the journey of the moon

> Circling around the red pavilion,
> Stooping at the silk-screened door,
> The moon shines on those who lie sleepless.

These lines anticipate Donne's question asked in "The Sunne Rising":

> Busie old foole, unruly Sunne,
> Why dost thou thus,
> Through windowes, and through curtaines call on us?

The device found in Hsin's lyrics, which allows for the human spirit to roam the universe, or to hold imaginary conversation with departed souls, is an expression of this kind of metaphysical wit, more akin to the humor of Li Po and Su Shih (who also are the subject of Poem 36) than to the allegorical style of *Li Sao*.

[POEM 35]

Tune title: Song of Magnolia Blossoms (Slow)
(*Mu-lan-hua man*)
Title: At Mid-Autumn Festival, I was drinking till dawn. Among the guests, someone remarked that there had been many poems written on people's waiting for the moonrise, but there had never been any poem written to send the moon off. Thereupon, I thought of using the "Heavenly Questions" (*T'ien-wen*) style [of Ch'ü Yüan] and wrote this poem.
Date of composition: Undetermined

I pity the moon tonight:
Where does it go
On this far journey?
Perhaps there's another world
Seen only from the other side,   5
East of the shadow?
It must be beyond the heavens—
In the vast void
Except for the great wind sending the Mid-Autumn off.
A mirror in flight has no roots: then who's to secure it in place?   10
The Goddess of the Moon is never married: then who's to keep her?

Say it traverses the bottom of the sea: then I ask for what?
So dim and blurred, it should make one grieve.
I fear that the long, long whale,
Splashing in the sea, would smash and shatter   15
Its jade palace and crystal towers.

The toad could certainly stand being bathed in water:
But let me ask if the jade rabbit knows how to sink and float?
If it can be said that all will come out whole and sound,
Then why does it gradually become a hook?   20

[AL 459]

[POEM 36]
Tune title: Prelude to Water Music (*Shui-tiao-ko-t'ou*)
Title: Chao Ch'ang-fu, on the fifteenth day of the
seventh month, sent me a poem which he
wrote by using Tung-p'o's [Su Shih's]
rhymes, and also alluding to the events in
the lives of Tung-p'o and T'ai-po [Li Po].
The poem is full of praise which I do not
deserve; he also agreed to a visit with me
at Ch'iu-shui. On the fourteenth day of
the eighth month, I was lying ill at Po-shan
Monastery. So I used his rhymes and
wrote this to thank him, and also to have
a copy sent to Wu Tzu-ssu.
Date of composition: (conj.) 1196–1200

My mind set on the vastness of space,
I once dreamed of ascending to the heavens—
          To fondle the white moon,
And spend an eternity watching over the world.   5
A guest arrived on a pair of phoenix-birds,
Said he had met "Green Mountain" and "Red Cliff"
Who invited me to climb up with them to the lofty cold.
Pouring the wine, reaching for the Big Dipper,
          I, the unworthy one, also among them.
A small song, I sang: 10
          "How my mind has wandered,
          "But how my body is inclined to sleep!
          "Like the Great Swan, one, two, took to the
                    lofty air,
          "And saw the heaven and the earth, the round and
                    the square."
Wishing to sing the tune a second time, I woke from my dream; 15
Pushing away my pillow, I, forlorn, pondered to myself:
Where lie the eclipse and the perfection of human affairs?
          There is a Fair One with whom I can talk,
          But the autumn river separates me from the Lady of the Moon.

[AL 356]

IV   *Poetry of Allusion*

The next three poems will focus more closely on Hsin Ch'i-chi's use of philosophy in his longer lyrics. Not only is the content of these poems deeply imbued with philosophical ideas—in itself a departure from the norm of lyric poetry—but the style of writing also marks a breakthrough, recognized as Hsin's distinctive contribution even in the poet's lifetime. Hsin's special technique and achievement, it seems, is derived from a familiarity with the ancient classics that permits him, not just to make allusions to isolated passages from them (which most Chinese poets do), but to quote verbatim his favorite passages of prose and to weave them into his poetry.

A common characteristic of Chinese prose is the prevalent use of the so-called particles, or nonconcrete words (*hsü-tzu*), words which have no meaning in themselves but lend expressiveness to the language, nonetheless, in quite specific ways. Certain particles that function adverbially or introduce a question (*ho* or *ch'i*, for example) are an accepted part of Chinese poetic vocabulary; but there is a special class of particles occurring at the end of a sentence in classical Chinese prose which, except for Han Yü's "ancient poetry" (*ku-shih*), has never been effectively used by Chinese poets before Hsin's time. There are many such terminal particles, including, for example, *che* (to indicate "one who" or "that which"), *yeh* (to mark an end of a declarative sentence), *i* (to mark an end of an exclamatory sentence or a sentence stating a completed action or a strong opinion), *hu* or *tsai* (to indicate a real or a rhetorical question), and *erh-i* (meaning something like "after all" or "that is all there is to be said"). In Hsin's poetry, however, these nonconcrete words, coming as they do at the end of a line, become, not a source of hindrance or annoyance, but a well-integrated device to add a kind of rhetorical force to the entire composition. It is his success in this direction that led later critics, probably out of mixed motives, to call his lyrica *tz'u-lun* (lyric discourses), "discourse" being a subgenre of Chinese prose. In other words, Hsin is said to have invented a style of his own, a type of discursive poetry, somewhat in the manner of Lucretius' *De Rerum Natura.* (See especially the lyric, to the tune of *Ho-hsin-lang,* written on the subject of the Stilled Clouds Pavilion, beginning with a line borrowed verbatim from *The Analects*: *shen-i wu shuai i,* but with the second intensifier-particle *i* supplied by Hsin.)

Hsin' Ch'i-chi's use of the *Chuang-tzu* is more frequent and more imaginative than his use of *The Analects*. And since the poetic quality of the Taoist work is outstanding, he does not hesitate to adapt whole passages from the *Chuang-tzu,* as he does so successfully in the second half of Poem 37. The poem, written in the longest *tz'u* pattern he ever used, is clearly a *tour de force.* Not only does Hsin effectively incorporate long passages of Chuang Tzu's prose, from the chapter of "Autumn Floods," but he also makes use of several other major strands of thought taken from the other chapters of the same book. The three passages (A–C) from the *Chuang-tzu* cited below (verbatim borrowings are indicated by italics) pertain to a main tenet of Chuang Tzu's thought; namely, the relativity of all things. The parable about the snail (Passage A) is used by the Taoist philosopher to explain the wastefulness and the ultimate insignificance of all wars. The fable about the huge bird called the "roc" and the little dove (Passage B) illustrate the folly of making pretensions about what one knows.

Passage A: (cf. lines 1–5 of Poem 37), from "Tze-yang" chapter of the *Chuang-tzu:*

Hui Tzu . . . introduced Tai Chin-jen to the ruler. Tai Chin-jen said, "There is a creature called the snail—does Your Majesty know it?"

"Yes."

"On top of its left horn is a kingdom called Buffet [Ch'u], and on top of its right horn is a kingdom called Maul* [Man]. At times they quarrel over territory and go to war, strewing the field with corpses by the ten thousand, the victor pursuing the vanquished for half a month before returning home."

"Pooh!" said the ruler. "What kind of empty talk is this?"

"But Your Majesty will perhaps allow me to show you the truth in it. Do you believe that there is a limit to the four directions, to up and down?" [23]

Passage B: (cf. lines 11–12 of Poem 37) from "Free and Easy Wandering" chapter of the *Chuang-tzu:*

In the northern darkness there is a fish and his name is K'un [meaning fish roe]. The K'un is so huge I don't know how many *li* he measures. He changes and becomes a bird whose name is P'eng. The back of the P'eng measures I don't know how many thousand *li* across and, when

---

* Watson's note: "I borrow these translations of the names with gratitude from Waley (*Three Ways of Thought,* p. 64)."

he rises up and flies off, his wings are like clouds all over the sky. . . .
He beats the whirlwind and rises ninety thousand *li*, setting off on the
sixth-month gale. . . .

The cicada and the little dove laugh at this, saying, "When we make
an effort and fly up, we can get as far as the elm or the sapanwood tree,
but sometimes we don't make it and just fall down on the ground. Now
how is anyone going to go ninety thousand *li* to the south!"

If you go off to the green woods nearby, you can take along food for
three meals and come back with your stomach as full as ever. If you
are going a hundred *li*, you must grind your grain the night before; and
if you are going a thousand *li*, you must start getting the provisions
together three months in advance. *What do these two creatures understand?* [24]

The next passage (C) not only provides the main theme of Poem
37 but is also the chief source of its imagery. The entire section of
Chuang Tzu's prose contains an allegory of pride, as seen in the attitude and speeches of the Lord of the River, the pride of intellectual
pretension. Although in both idea and language, the poetic quality
of the original is very much evident, a close comparison of Hsin's
lyric with the *Chuang-tzu* text can further reveal the poet's insight
and his skill at recombination.

Passage C: The time of the autumn floods came and the *hundred streams
poured into the Yellow River. Its racing current swelled to
such proportions that, looking from bank to bank or island to
island, it was impossible to distinguish* a horse from a cow.
*Then the Lord of the River was beside himself with joy,
believing that all the beauty in the world belonged to him
alone.* Following the current, he *journeyd east until at last he
reached the North Sea. Looking east,* he could see no end to
the water.

The Lord of the River began to wag his head and roll his
eyes. Peering far off *in the direction of Jo* [the god of the
sea], *he sighed and said,* "The common saying has it, 'He has
heard the Way a mere hundred times but he thinks he's better
than anyone else.' It applies to me. In the past, I heard men
belittling the learning of Confucius and making light of the
righteousness of Po Yi, though I never believed them. Now,
however, I have seen your unfathomable vastness. *If I hadn't
come to your gate, I wou'd have been in danger. I would
forever have been laughed at by the masters of the Great
Method!"* [25]

[POEM 37]

Tune title: A Slow Chant (*Shao-pien*)
Title: Pavilion of Autumn Floods (*Ch'iu-shui Kuan*)
Date of composition: 1199

Inside the horn of a snail, a battle rages between
Two kingdoms: Ch'u to the left and Man to the right.
A single combat extends o'er a thousand *li* of ground.
    Try to imagine
This feeble heart encased in an inch of space!   5
Indeed, all emptiness is contained in infinitude.
    If this truth be known,
Who can tell between Mount T'ai and a single hair?
From ancient times, heaven and earth lie in a grain of rice.
    Ah, knowing the small resemble the great,   10
    A turtledove or a roc is happy with its own fate.
What else can these two creatures know?
Remember, if Robber Chih had led a moral and just life, Confucius
    would have been proved wrong;
Not to mention Infant Shang blessed with longevity and old P'eng-
    tsu ending his life in sadness.
To expound on cold with rats unafraid of fire,   15
Or to talk of heat with silkworms thriving on ice:
Who can tell between likenesses and differences?

    Ah!
Time decides what's noble and what's base;
Priceless jade could only fetch a sheepskin.   20
Who's able, then, to make all things equal?
    In my dream, I beheld Chuang Chou
Tidying up the lost chapters of his writing
And looking at me with a skittish smile.
In my empty pavilion, I woke and named it "Autumn Floods."   25
    A guest arrived to ask about the Great River,
Which a hundred streams had swollen with rain,
While raging currents merged water with land's banks;
Whereupon the Lord of the River was transported with joy,
Believing that all beauty of the world belonged to him alone.   30
    Across the distant deep,
He turned his gaze eastward to the ocean;
Timorously bowed to the God of the Sea and, in amazement, sighed:
    Saying, "If I had not met you,
    Among all Masters of Great Truth, I would not   35
Have escaped being laughed at through eternity, after all!"

How much water can this pavilion of mine boast of?
　Only a clear stream,
　One tiny bend, that's all!

[AL 342]

Hsin Ch'i-chi's effective use of the original sources lies not only in the skillful adaptation of entire passages, as he does in line 12 and in lines 29–30 of the above poem, but also in the deletions and additions he made. For instance, from the anecdote about the encounter between the Lord of the River and the God of the Sea, which in the original is told in over ninety words, Hsin takes about half of them and adds to these some words of his own, paraphrasing the rest. Among the changes or deletions are: the use of "rain" in place of "river" in line 27 and the omission of the reference to "horse and cow," in line 28, instead of which two words he picks up the words "from bank to bank" (*ssu* and *ya*) of the previous line in the *Chuang-tzu*. This change, certainly, could not have been due to squeamishness, for in another lyric of Hsin's he actually begins the poem with the lines: "Some thought I was a cow;/ Another thought I was a horse,"[26] which are also lines taken verbatim from the *Chuang-tzu*. But we must admit that the deletion here gains in relevancy and directness as far as the poem is concerned. Words added by Hsin are either modifiers or particles; such as "in amazement" (*ching*) before "sighed," in line 33; or "timorously" (*ch'ün-hsün*, a rhymed compound) before "bowed," in the same line; or the particle meaning "after all" (*erh*, which is also a rhyme word for that line). Alterations such as these reveal not only the fruits of his reading but also his concern for the coherence and unity of the entire poem. Like Shakespeare's use of Plutarch, Hsin's borrowings from the *Chuang-tzu* reflect a desire "to dress old words new."

V *A Companion Poem*

Poem 38 bears the title: "Written by Using the Rhyme [words] of the Previous Poem." The practice of duplicating in a new poem the rhyme words of another poem, composed earlier either by oneself or by another person, is common with Chinese poets. The challenge in this kind of exercise, or this kind of social game, is that the poet has to think of new compounds or new meanings for the same rhyme words so that he will not produce a poem devoid of any new ideas. (In a translation, it is impossible to duplicate the rhyme words by using the same English words, or even to follow the sentence order exactly each time, especially since a word in Chinese may have several meanings; for instance, *li*, a rhyme word in line 3, means "a Chinese mile" (as in Poem 37), but *li* is used in Poem 38 in the compound of *t'ien-li*, which means "farm." However, in the Notes to Poem 38, I shall point out all the words in my translation of the two poems which correspond to the rhyme words in the original.)

This companion poem, when compared with Poem 37 (which is *its* original), may be found to be less descriptive and more discursive, since it lacks the "frame" of a "dream-allegory." However, even when the separate images of the poem are derived from at least four unrelated passages (D–G) from the *Chuang-tzu* (shorter passages of allusions will be given in the Notes), they are unified by a common theme of contentment versus envy, and of self-knowledge. Passage D describes the corrupting effects of envy with a fable about a *k'uei's* encounter with the millepede, while Passage F tells about the disastrous consequences for foxes and leopards valued for the beauty of their fur or skin. Passage E tells a story which warns that when disaster strikes, what is the cause of the disaster holds very little significance.

Passage D: (cf. line 15 and the word "Awakening" (*chi*) in line 30 of (Poem 38) from "Autumn Floods" chapter of the *Chuang-tzu*:

The K'uei [a being with only one leg] *envies the millepede*, the millepede envies the snake, the snake envies the wind, the wind envies the eye, and the eye envies the mind.

The K'uei said to millepede, "I have this one leg that I hop along on, though I make little progress. Now how in the world do you manage to work all those ten thousand legs of yours?" . . .

The snake said, "It's just the heavenly mechanism [*chi*] moving me along . . ." [27]

Passage E: (cf. line 16) from "Webbed Toes" chapter of the *Chuang-tzu*:

The slave boy [Tsang] and the slave girl [Ku] were out together herding their sheep, and both of them lost their flocks. Ask the slave boy how it happened: well, he had a bundle of writing slips and was reading a book. Ask the slave girl how it happened: well, she was playing a game of toss-and-wait-your-turn. They went about the business in different ways, but in losing their sheep they were equal.[28]

Passage F: (cf. line 20) from "The Mountain Tree" chapter of the
    Chuang-tzu:

The Master from south of the Market said, "Your technique for
avoiding disaster is a very superficial one. *The sleek-furred fox and the
elegantly spotted leopard* dwell in the mountain forest and crouch in
the cliffside caves—such is their quietude. They go abroad by night
but lurk at home by day—such is their caution. . . . And yet they can't
seem to escape the disaster of nets and traps. Where is the *blame?*
Their *fur* is their undoing.[29]

The final selection from the *Chuang-tzu* (Passage G), quoted below, is a humorous account of the supposed meeting between the
Taoist philosopher and Hui Tzu, a philosopher of the School of
Logicians, who was beaten at the game in a "pseudological debate."
The story, which unfolds in a series of word-play and ends by de-
fining the limits of logical knowledge, holds a tremendous appeal
for Hsin Ch'i-chi.

Passage G: (cf. lines 33–34) from "Autumn Floods" chapter of the
    Chuang-tzu:

Chuang Tzu and Hui Tzu were strolling along the dam of the Hao
River when Chuang Tzu said, "See how the minnows come out and dart
around where they please! That's what fish really enjoy!"
    Hui Tzu said, "You're not a fish—how do you know what fish enjoy?"
    Chuang Tzu said, "You're not I, so how do you know I don't know
what fish enjoy?"
    Hui Tzu said, *"I'm not you,* so I certainly don't know what you know.
On the other hand, you're certainly not a fish—so that still proves you
don't know what fish enjoy!"
    Chuang Tzu said, "Let's go back to your original question, please.
You asked me *how* I know what fish enjoy—so you already knew I
knew it when you asked the question. I know it by standing here beside
the Hao." [30]

[POEM 38]

Tune title: A Slow Chant (*Shao-pien*)
Title: Written by Using the Rhyme [words]
of the Previous Poem
Date of composition: 1199

A single valley to call one's own
"Five Willows" can laugh,
His waning years spent on the farm.

I ask who knows
Smallest stirrings of the infinite? 5
I gaze at wild geese in flight,
Distant and dark, at horizon's edge.
Speaking of the subtle truth,
Coarse wine is just right to sustain my long thirst.
From now on, I must ferment the rice I grow myself.
Alas! beauty and ugliness are hard to equate, 10*
Nor fullness and emptiness succeeding each other.
Must Heaven be scrutable to men?
Look back: my fifty-nine years are all misspent.
Like pleasures dreamt of in dream—upon waking, sad.
K'uei, with one leg, envies the millepede; 15
Ku, the wastrel, also lost his sheep.
In the final count, what difference?

Ah!
Taboo of things lies in their extremity:
Thick-coated fox and striped leopard are doomed by their pelt. 20
Wealth and honor are not among my desires;
Then, where are you headed—so distracted and nervous?
Now, the myriad noises are silenced,
With the moon bright in the midnight sky;
And my heart, ten thousand miles away, clear as a stream. 25
Though I feel my spirit has roamed far and wide,
I return to where I sit, staring at
The hazy banks of River Huai:
When once I see fish and birds happy in their forgetting,
I know I've forgotten my Awakening as well as myself. 30
When have I ever
Viewed myself and realized the "thingness" in me?
If such weren't the cherished sentiment of the minnows on Hao River,
It must be because "I am not you."
The Lord of the River need not blush before the God of the Sea; 35
Small or great, they are both made of water, after all!
What cause is there in life for joy or rancor?
I laugh at the Master
Thrice an official, thrice dismissed!

[AL 344]

---

* For ease of comparison with Poem 37, I have counted lines 6-7 of this poem as one line, following Poem 37. The variation is explained in the Notes to Poems.

Throughout this poem, the tone is entirely personal and the emotion genuine, although the paradoxes used were originally written down by an ancient philosopher over fifteen hundred years ago. The literary allusions are limited to two instances, both referring to T'ao Ch'ien, known as the "Master of Five Willows"; the line, "wealth and honor are not among my desires" (line 22), is borrowed verbatim from T'ao Ch'ien's rhyme-prose composition "Let's Go Home" (*Kuei-ch'ü-lai-tz'u*).[31] There is another verbatim quotation, in line 5, this time from the *I ching,* a classic popular with Sung Neo-Confucianists, which might have shown Hsin his "manifest destiny" if the story about his use of the book in his youth were to be believed. And the poem ends with a specific reference to his official career, that he has been "retired" three times by the court; this mention is, of course, concealed, in an allusion to *The Analects* (V: 19).[32] The story from *The Analects* tells about a model minister named Tzu-wen, praised by Confucius as having been "certainly faithful to his prince's interests" by showing no elation during each of the three times he was appointed to office and no bitterness during each of the three times he was dismissed. Thus, it is all by means of ancient "matere" that Hsin tells a personal story, a poem of wit and charm and also of great poignancy.

A modern Welsh poet, David Jones, commenting on "the artist's horizon," has said that an artist will find "material of which it could be said

> '. . . in scole is gret altercacioun
> In this matere, and gret disputision'

and, although it is absolutely incumbent upon the artist to use this disputed 'matere,' he . . . has not infrequently to say . . . 'Those been the cokkes wordes and not myne.' "[33] Jones characterizes the work of an artist as, not in being "a seer or endowed with the gift of prophecy," but in being "something of a vicar . . . [or] legatine . . . to deliver what has been delivered to him, who can neither add to nor take from the deposits."[34] "There is only one tale to tell," Jones writes, "even though the telling is patient of endless development and ingenuity and can take on a million variant forms. I imagine something of this sort to be implicit in what Picasso is reported as saying: 'I do not seek, I find.' "[35] Hsin Ch'i-chi is this kind of an artist.

VI   *Hsin's Last Poem*

As a final selection from Hsin Ch'i-chi's poetry, I quote a poem which might not have been the last poem he ever wrote; but it was, according to the title, written within two months of his death. Typically, the lyric is deeply imbued with the Taoist philosophy, garnished at the same time with an allusion to the works of a Neo-Confucian philosopher of the Northern Sung period. The style is erudite and yet urbane—a "mournful melody" from "accomplished fingers"—and his eyes, "amid many wrinkles," in the words of William Butler Yeats, his "ancient, glittering eyes are gay."

[POEM 39]

> Tune title: Song of Grotto Fairy [*Tung-hsien-ko*]
> Title: Written in the Eighth Month of *Ting-mao*
> [1207] While Ill

        Between a sage and a fool
        Calculate: how small a distance!
A difference in centimeters, an error of a thousand miles.
        Weighed by the grains:
The distinction between right and profit, Emperor and Thief—   5
        Tireless do-gooders
        Are all those who rise at cock's crow.

        Sweet-flavored things spoil too easily—
        Only in my waning years I know:
        True friendship is limpid as water.   10
        One drop of food invites mosquitoes
        With their thundering chant.
        How starkly I feel:
        Yesterday's untruth, today's verity!
How I'd like a cup of Serendipity Soup from the Nest of Peace and Joy,
        Which I can drink heartily and without default,   15
        Just to get half-drunk—that's all!

                                        [AL 540]

As an artist, Hsin Ch'i-chi knows that poetry is ultimately, and inherently, derived from a tradition that is older than itself; that lyric poetry, whatever its origin and conventions, must express what is in one's heart; and that the final measure of a poet's achievement lies in the control of his medium, which is language. How he fared in all these areas has been the story of this book.

Notes and References

Abbreviations of Titles and Editions

Works by Hsin Ch'i-chi

PP   *Chia-hsüan shih-wen ch'ao-ts'un* [The Poems and Prose of Chia-hsüan], ed. Teng Kuang-ming (Shanghai, 1947).

AL   *Chia-hsüan tz'u pien-nien ch'ien-chu* [The Annotated Lyrics of Chia-hsüan Arranged in Chronological Order], ed. Teng Kuang-ming (Shanghai, 1957; 1962).

Frequently Cited Works in the Notes

CKT   *Chan-kuo ts'e* [Strategies of the Warring States], SPPY.

CS   *Chin shih* [History of the Chin (1122–1234) Dynasty], by T'uo [K'e]-t'uo (*ca.* early fourteenth century).

CSCC   *Chin-shu chiao-chu* [Annotated and Corrected Edition of the History of the Chin (265–420) Dynasty], by Fan Hsüan-Ling (578–648) *et al.*

CST   *Ch'üan Sung tz'u* [Complete Sung Lyrics], ed. T'ang Kuei-chang.

CTS   *Ch'üan T'ang shih* [Complete T'ang Poetry].

CTS (Liu)   *Chiu T'ang shu* [Old History of T'ang] by Liu Hsü (887–946).

HTCTC   *Hsü tzu-chih t'ung-chien* [Continuation of the Comprehensive Mirror of Perfect Administration], by Pi Yüan.

HTS   *Hsin T'ang shu* [New History of T'ang] by Ou-yang Hsiu.

LTMCTI   *Li-tai ming-ch'en tsou-i* [Memorials of Famous Ministers of Successive Dynasties], compiled by Huang Huai *et al.*

NP   *Hsin Chia-hsüan nien-p'u* [Chronology of the Life of Hsin Chia-hsüan], by Teng Kuang-ming.

NSWLL	*Nan-Sung wen-lü lü* [Record of Prose Works of Southern Sung Dynasty].
SCPMHP	*San-ch'ao pei-meng hui-pien* [Collectanea of Records of Treatises with the North During Three Reigns [(1117–62)], by Hsü Meng-hua (1126–1207).
SHYCK	*Sung-hui-yao chi-kao* [A Compilation of State Regulations of Sung), by Hsü Sung.
SS	*Sung shih* [History of Sung Dynasty], T'uo [K'e]-t'uo (*ca.* early fourteenth century).
SSHY	*Shih-shuo hsin-yü* [A New Account of the Tales of the World], by Liu I-ch'ing (403–44).
THTP	*Tz'u-hua ts'ung-pien* [Collectanea of Talks on *Tz'u*].
Ting	*Ch'üan Han San-kuo Chin Nan-Pei-ch'ao shih* [Complete Poetry of Han, Three Kingdoms, Chin, and the Northern and Southern Dynasties], ed. Ting-Fu-pao.
YTCS	*Yü-ti chi-sheng* [Records of Famous Sites on the Empire], by Wang Hsiang-chih (Preface dated 1221).

Editions

SPPY	*Ssu-pu pei-yao* [Essentials of the Four Libraries].
SPTK	*Ssu-pu ts'ung-k'an* [The Four Libraries].
TSCC	*Ts'ung-shu chi-ch'eng* [Collection of Collections of Works].

Chapter One

1. The translation of *tz'u* as "Lyric Metres" is proposed by James J. Y. Liu in *The Art of Chinese Poetry* (Chicago, 1962), p. 30. Alternative translations of this term are "song-poems," used by James R. Hightower in *Topics of Chinese Literature* (Cambridge, 1950), p. 80, and "poems in irregular metre," suggested by Cyril Birch in *Anthology of Chinese Literature* (New York, 1965), p. 333. For fuller explanations of these terms, see Chapter 2.

2. See *chüan* 23 of *Hsing-shih heng-yen* [Lasting Words to Awaken the World], a compilation of 1627, ed. Feng Meng-lung (1574–1646).

3. Yüan Hao-wen (1190–1257), *Chung-chou chi,* SPTK edition, 3/13b. Hsin's official biography in the SS gives the name of Ts'ai Sung-nien (Ts'ai Po-chien, 1107–1159) as "the teacher of Tang-Hsin" (401/1a). But this account appears dubious in that Ts'ai was a prominent official in the court of the Chin empire and assumed the prime ministership under Prince Hai-ling, who came to power in 1149. Most modern critics, except Hu Shih, believe that Yüan's account is the more reliable.

4. The *I Ching,* trans. Cary Baynes from the German version of Richard Wilhelm (New York, 1950), 2 vols., II, 173–78.

5. *Ibid.,* II, 178–82.

6. *Ibid.,* II, 181.

7. *Ibid.,* II, 180.

8. *Ibid.,* II, 182.

9. *Ibid.,* I, iv.

10. SS, 401/1b.

11. Ch'en Liang, "Inscription on a Portrait of Hsin Chia-hsüan," *Lung-ch'uan wen-chi,* TSCC edition, 10/102b.

12. Hung Mai, "Chia-hsüan chi," in NSWLL, 10/17b. Also reprinted in Supplement "One" to PP, la.

13. The date of 1165 is purely conjectural, suggested by the editor Huang Huai (1367–1449) of LTMCTI, where the text (94/1a–22b) is prefaced with the statement that these essays were presented by Hsin while he was serving as the Signatory Official of Chien-k'ang. Huang's dating is said to be based upon the Yung-lo Encyclopedia (*Yung-lo ta-tien,* compiled 1403, now lost), but modern scholars believe that the internal evidences supplied by the text suggest a later date, probably 1168.

14. NSWLL, 11/16b–17b; also reprinted in NP, 36.

15. An excerpt from this rhyme-prose composition is given in Chiang Lin-chu, *Hsin Ch'i-chi chuan* [Biography of Hsin Ch'i-chi] (Taipei, 1964), p. 60. The original appears in *chüan* 1 of Chou Fu, *Tu-chai ch'ien-tao-pien* [Chapters from a Blunt Knife of a Bookworm's Studio].

16. NP, 35–36.

17. SHYCK, 3731.

18. PP, 34–35; LTMCTI, 272/13a–14b.

19. Sung civil officials were classified in nine ranks, actually eighteen since each rank consisted of two categories: "full" (*cheng*) and "associate" (*tsung*). SS, 401/4b.

20. PP, 35–37; LTMCTI, 319/15a–16b.

21. SS, 401/3b–4a.

22. SS gives the number of "two tiles" per family, but Lo Ta-ching (*fl.* 1224), in describing one of Hsin's building projects, records that the poet once requisitioned "twenty tiles per family" by offering cash for them and was thus able to gather a more than adequate supply in two days (*Ho-lin yü-lu,* 12/2b). The number of "twenty" might be more believable if this account refers to the same project.

23. Passages from a dozen contemporary accounts relating to this topic of the Flying Tigers Army are given on pages 64–70 of NP.

24. *Chu-wen-kung wen-chi,* SPTK edition, 21/26a–26b.

25. The eight words are: *pi-ti* [a misprint for *t'iao*]-*che-p'ei; ch'iang-*

ti-che-chan, according to SS, 401/4a. But this episode is also recorded in *Chu-tzu yü-lei* [Classified Conversation of Master Chu], quoted in NP 73. Hsin's order was said by Chu Hsi to have consisted of the following eight words: *chieh-ho-che-chan; pi-t'iao-che-p'ei;* namely, "He who robs others of grain will be executed; he who refuses to sell rice to others will be conscripted." Chu could have recalled this from memory.

26. SS, 401/4b, where this censure is said to have been lodged after Hsin's term of office in Fukien. SHYCK, p. 4004, dates this censure in 1181. Teng's conjectural emendation of the date, NP, p. 81, is probably correct.

27. SS, 401/4b.

28. HTCTC, pp. 152, 4063–64.

29. *The Analects,* XIV: 1.

30. YTCS, 21/1a, 2b, and 3a.

31. NSWLL, 10/17b–18a; also reproduced in PP, Supplement "One," 1–2. Hsin's attachment to agriculture is well known. The official biography mentions that he once said: "People in North China seek self-sufficiency; therefore, there are not very rich or very poor people. On the other hand, the people in the South are fond of engaging in superfluous activities (*mo-tso*) designed to harm farmers and to exploit them; hence, there are rich people and poor people" (401/5b). All nine sons of the poet, except one who died early, were given names written with the radical for "wheat" (*ho*).

32. Ch'en Liang, "Letter to Compiler Hsin Yu-an," *op. cit.,* 21/257.

33. A quotation from T'ao Ch'ien, "Tu Shan-hai-ching, No. 1," *Ching-chieh hsien-sheng chi,* SPPY edition, 4/13a.

34. A direct quotation attributed to Yü K'ai (262–311), who tried to befriend Wang Yen, a man known for his uprightness and love for "pure talk" (*ch'ing-t'an*), by addressing him with the familiar pronoun "you" (*ch'ing*) instead of the more polite *chün.* The story comes from *Shih-shuo hsin-yü,* 3/76b.

35. The text reads *Ch'in,* the name of China's first empire (221–207 B.C.), known for its military prowess. It is used rather loosely by Hsin to refer to his place of origin, which is Shantung in the northeast. "Northwest" agrees only with the earlier paragraph.

36. A reference to Chia I (201–169 B.C.), banished to Changsha after a brilliant political career in his early youth. He wished to offer his service in repelling the powerful Hsiung-nu, which threatened Han China from the north, but his ambition was thwarted and he died in exile. Among his writings was a rhyme-prose composition lamenting the death of Ch'ü Yüan, the ancient poet who died in political exile.

37. A reference to 1. 31 of "Summoning the Spirits" (*Chao-hun*), in *The Songs of Ch'u.* The entire line, in David Hawkes's translation (p.

105), reads: "For tigers and leopards guard the gates, with jaws ever ready to rend up mortal men."

38. Implying a supplication, though humorously put, for favorable omens and the need to curb all desires. According to the *Vimalakirti-nirdesa-sutra,* an immensely popular Buddhist scripture in China which had three translations between the third and the seventh century, the Heavenly Maiden revealed herself in Vimalakirti's cell upon hearing the latter expound the scriptures.

39. "A Reply to Hsin Yu-an," Chu, *op. cit.,* 85/26b.

40. HTCTC, 155/4176.

41. SS, 401/6a.

42. See the translator's Introduction to *Reflections on Things at Hand: The Neo-Confucian Anthology,* compiled by Chu Hsi and Lü Tsu-ch'ien, trans., with notes, Wing-tsit Chan (New York, Columbia University Press, 1967).

Chapter Two

1. Kaj Birket-Smith, *The Eskimos* (London: Methuen, 1936, 1959; Danish edition, 1927), p. 68.

2. Fujio Koyama, *Chinese Ceramics* (Tokyo: Nikon Keizai, 1960), p. 12.

3. James J. Y. Liu, *The Art of Chinese Poetry,* p. 30.

4. Hsü Shen, *Shuo-wen chieh-tzu chu,* 9/29a–b.

5. This *tz'u* has the denotative meaning of "words," to be distinguished from *yen* which means "language." See Achilles Fang's note to this word (pp. 560–61) in his "Rhymeprose on Literature: The *Wen-fu* of Lu Chi (A.D. 261–303)," *Harvard Journal of Asiastic Studies,* XIV (1951), 527–66; reprinted in John L. Bishop, ed., *Studies in Chinese Literature* (Cambridge, 1965), pp. 3–42. The meaning of *tz'u* as "embellishment" occurs in such compounds as *tz'u-tsao;* cf. Lu Chi, *Wen-fu,* cited above, 1. 13.

6. "Collective Biography of Scholars" ("Ju-lin lieh-chuan"), *Shih chi* (Peking: Chung Hua, 1959), p. 3121, where the word *tz'u* that later came to mean "lyrics" is used in the compound *wen-tz'u* to mean "literature."

7. Glen W. Baxter, "Metrical Origins of the *Tz'u,"* in Bishop, *op. cit.,* pp. 203 ff.

8. In a letter to G. W. Baxter, Arthur Waley indicated his preference for "melody-type" to "tune-pattern" as a rendering of *tiao;* see Bishop, p. 223.

9. See Jacques Gernet, *Daily Life in China on the Eve of the Mongol Invasion, 1250–1276,* trans. H. M. Wright (New York, 1962).

10. SS, 164/17b–18a; also 129/2b.

11. Chou Mi, *Ch'i-tung yeh-yü* [Words of a Fool from Ch'i-tung], Han-feng Lou ed., 19 *chüan*, 10/10b.

12. Rulan Chao Pian, *Sonq Dynasty Musical Sources and Their Interpretation* (Cambridge, 1967), pp. 99–129. See especially the extant Sung musical scores for seventeen lyrics by Chiang K'uei [Jiang Kwei] (*ca.* 1155–*ca.* 1235) written by the poet himself and transcribed into Western notation by Pian.

13. *Ch'in-ting tz'u-p'u* [The Imperial Register of *Tz'u* Prosodies], compiled during the reign period of Ch'ien-lung (1736–96) lists 826 tune titles and a total of 2,306 variants; while Wan Shu (*fl.* 1692), *Tz'u-lü*, a handbook for the writing of *tz'u* (Preface dated 1687), lists 875 tune titles and a total of 1,675 variants. See Liu, *op. cit.*, p. 30.

14. James R. Hightower, *Topics in Chinese Literature*, p. 80.

15. Cyril Birch, ed., *Anthology of Chinese Literature: from Early Times to the Fourteenth Century* (New York: Grove Press, 1965), p. 333.

16. Liu, *op. cit.*, p. 30.

17. It is also known as the *Classic of Poetry,* as *Book of Odes* (B. Karlgren), as *Confucian Odes* (Ezra Pound), or as *Book of Songs* (Arthur Waley).

18. The title of this anthology, in David Hawkes's translation, is given as *Ch'u Tz'u: the Songs of the South* (London, 1959, 1962).

19. For a fuller discussion of these poetic devices, see Chapters 1–4 in Liu, *op. cit.*, pp. 3–47.

20. R. Poggioli, "Formalism," in Shipley's *Dictionary of World Literature* (New York: The Philosophical Library, 1943), p. 254.

21. Quoted in René Wellek and Austin Warren, *Theory of Literature* (New York: Harcourt, Brace, 1942, 1949), p. 246.

22. *Ibid.*

23. Liu, *op. cit.*, p. 96.

24. Actually, the earliest printed edition (1299) of Hsin Ch'i-chi's collected works is known by the title of *Chia-hsüan ch'ang-tuan-chü,* which is also the title recorded in *I-wen-chih* ("Bibliography Section") of SS, 208/23a.

25. See Wan Shu, *Tz'u-lü,* Preface, SPPY edition, 1a-1b. These terms originate from an anonymous editor of a *tz'u* anthology known to have been compiled before 1200.

26. *Yü-t'ai hsin-yung* [New Songs of Jade Pavilion], SPPY edition, 10/16b. Hsiao Kang, Emperor Chien-wen of the Liang Kingdom (*r.* 550–51) during the Six Dynasties period.

27. *Ibid.,* 10/10b.

28. CTS, p. 4519.

29. *Li T'ai-po ch'üan-chi,* SPPY edition, 5/12a.

30. CTS, p. 4129.

31. *Hua-chien chi* [Among-the-flowers Collection], SPPY edition, 2/4a. For *ch'ih,* the text in this edition reads *ti,* a misprint.

32. *Ibid.,* 2/3a.

33. For a description of the prosodic schemes of T'ang poetry, see Liu, *op. cit.,* pp. 26–27.

34. Kenkichiro Kojima, *Chung-kuo wen-hsüeh t'ung-lun* [Essays on Chinese Literature], trans. Sun Liang-kung (Taipei: Commercial Press, 1965), p. 254.

35. Wan Shu, *Tz'u-lü,* 1/4a.

36. Wang Li, *Han-yü shih-lü hsüeh* [Prosody of Chinese Poetry], p. 11.

37. Liu, *op. cit.,* pp. 146–47.

38. *Ibid,* pp. 149–50.

39. Lu Chi, *Wen-fu,* 1. 43, in Achilles Fang's translation; Bishop, *op. cit.,* p. 12.

Chapter Three

1. *Ch'u Tz'u: The Songs of the South,* pp. 25, 32, and 33.

2. CTS, p. 512.

3. *Tung-p'o yüeh-fu,* 1/9b.

4. *Mao-chu-hsi shih-tz'u san-shih-ch'i shou* [Thirty-seven Poems of Chairman Mao] (Peking, 1964), p. 10a.

5. T. S. Eliot, *On Poetry and Poets* (New York: Farrar, Straus and Cudahy, 1943, 1957), p. 225.

6. *Ibid.*

7. *Ibid.,* p. 238.

8. *Ibid.,* p. 239.

9. *Shih ching,* "The Airs of Wei," No. 2, stanza 2, line 4; Arthur Waley, trans., *The Book of Songs* (No. 7), p. 24.

10. The passage is found in the "eulogy" (*tsan*) section in the chapter "Collective Biography of Chao Ch'ung-kuo (137–52 B.C.) and Hsin Ch'ing-chi (*d.* 12 B.C.)." Commenting on the fact that both of these generals and several others had come from Shansi, the historian Pan Ku ascribed this phenomenon to the martial spirit of the people of that region. Then he quoted a few lines of a chariot song from the state of Ch'in as evidence, and he added: "The customs and habits of the people there have been the same since ancient times; in the singing of those songs and sighing over them [*ko-yu k'ang-k'ai*] are still preserved the attitudes and bearings [*feng-liu*] of the people" (*Han shu,* p. 2999).

11. CSCC, 36/26b.

12. James J. Y. Liu, *The Chinese Knight-Errant* (Chicago: The University of Chicago Press, 1967), p. 56.

13. Yüeh K'o, *T'ing-shih*, 3/16b–19a.

14. *Han shu*, p. 2230.

15. Ch'en Shu-mei, *Chia-hsüan-tz'u yung-tien feng-lei yen-chiu* [A Classified Study of the Use of Allusions in the Lyrics of Chia-hsüan]. (M.A. thesis; Taipei: National Taiwan University, 1967), pp. 170–84.

16. *Ibid.*, p. 17.

17. In the Chinese text, Li Ts'ai is referred to as Li Kuang's *ts'ung-ti*, a term that designates a younger "brother" of the clan, or "first cousin on the father's side." *Hsia-chung* (lit., "the middle of the low") might be said to correspond to C in a letter-value scale from A-plus to C-minus. See *Shih chi*, p. 2873, and *Han shu*, p. 863.

18. Ch'en, *op. cit.*, pp. 18–19.

Chapter Four

1. Erza Pound, *The Confucian Ode* (New York, 1959), p. 142; *Shih ching*, Poem 229; Waley, *The Book of Songs*, No. 110.

2. J. D. Frodsham, *The Murmuring Stream* (Kuala Lumpur, 1967), I, 158.

3. "Drinking Wine, V," trans. Robert Kotewall and Norman L. Smith, *The Penguin Book of Chinese Verse* (Baltimore, 1962), p. 9.

4. Renato Poggioli, "The Oaten Flute," in *Perspectives on Poetry*, eds. James L. Calderwood and Harold E. Toliver (New York: Oxford University Press, 1968), p. 224.

5. *Ibid.*, p. 227.

6. *Lun-yü*, VI:9. The translation is by Arthur Waley, *The Analects of Confucius* (London: Allen & Unwin, 1938; reprinted in The Modern Library edition by Random House), pp. 117–18.

7. *Ibid.*, XVIII: 8. This term is translated by Waley as "subjects whose services were lost to the state"; *ibid.*, p. 221.

8. A title of similar import, used by the Buddhists, is *chü-shih*, which can mean, however, either a "layman who practices his faith at home" or "a wealthy benefactor."

9. Fung Yu-lan, *A Short History of Chinese Philosophy*, trans. Derk Bodde (New York: The Macmillan Company, 1948, 1960), p. 100.

10. Mai-mai Sze, *The Way of Chinese Painting* (New York: Bollingen, 1956; Random House, 1959), p. 17.

11. *Jen-chien tz'u-hua*, in the THTP, p. 4243.

12. "Chinese Buddhism," Fung Yu-lan has said, "must be distinguished from Buddhism in China." See Fung, *op. cit.*, p. 242.

13. *Ibid.*

14. For an example, see Yen Shu's (991–1055) line, "A lotus covered with dew are her two cheeks, and distant hills her eyebrows" (*lu-lien shuang-nien yüan-shan mei*), CST, p. 97.

15. Cheng Ch'ien, "Hsin Chia-hsüan yü Han T'o-chou," in *Ts'ung shih tao ch'ü* [From *Shih* to *Ch'ü*] (Tapei, n.d.), pp. 140–49.

16. Keats wrote, "We hate poetry that has a palpable design upon us" in Letter to J. H. Reynolds, February 3, 1818; see *The Letters of John Keats*, ed. H. E. Rollins, 2 vols. (Cambridge: Harvard University Press, 1958), I, 224.

17. *Ibid.*

Chapter Five

1. The matter of versification is appended here as a note, since it is too technical to be included in the text of this chapter. According to my tabulation, Hsin Ch'i-chi employs approximately 101 different "tune patterns"; and only twenty of these, or about one-fifth, are among the patterns used by the *Hua-chien* poets. The seven most frequently used patterns (over twenty lyrics for each) are listed below, in the order of decreasing incidence, showing the number of words required by each pattern (disregarding variants), the total number of lyrics composed in that tune in Hsin's works, and the rhyming scheme of each (for symbols used, see Chapter 2):

(1) *Che-ku-t'ien* (55 words; 63 poems)
   Pattern: 7A 7A 7 7A / 3 3A 7A 7 7
(2) *Shui-tiao-ko-t'ou* (95 words; 37 poems)
   Pattern: 5 5A 4 7A 6 6 5A 5 5A / 3 3 3A 4 7A 6 6 5A 5 5A
(3) *Man-chiang-hung* (93 words; 34 poems)
   Pattern: 4 3 4a 3 4 4a 7 7 3 5 3a / 3 3a 3 3a 5 4a 7 7a 3 5 3a
(4) *Lin-chiang-hsien* (60 words; 24 poems)
   Pattern: 7 6A 7A 5 5A / 76A 7A 5 5
(5) *Ho-hsin-lang* (116 words; 23 poems)
   Pattern: 5a 3 4 4a 7 6a 3 4a 7 3 5a 3 3a / 7a 3 4 4a 7 6a 3 4a 7 3 5a 3 3a
(6) *Nien-nu-chiao* (100 words; 22 poems)
   Pattern: 4 5 4a 7 6a 4 4 5a 4 6a / 6 4 5a 7 6a 4 4 5a 4 6a
(7) *P'u-sa-man* (44 words; 22 poems)
   Pattern: 7a 7a 5B 5B / 5c 5c 5D 5D

Of these *tz'u* patterns, "Che-ku-t'ien" is the only pattern that bears the closest resemblance to the traditional *shih* structure (of the four-line *chüeh-chü* and the eight-line *lü-shih* variety)—a fact which might indicate that it is easier to use than most of the other tunes. Yet even in this pattern, the two three-word lines (which replace a seven-word line) in the middle afford a greater flexibility than the prosodic structure of a poem in the "regulated verse," or *lü-shih,* meter.

It is an interesting phenomenon that many of the Sung poets, with the exception of Su Shih, were successful in handling only one of the two types of poetic composition, not both. Hsin's traditional poems (*shih*) were not much admired by his contemporaries, although he must have written a number of them. The first attempt to collect and print Hsin's traditional poems was not made until 1582, when Hsin Ch'i-t'ai copied down 110 poems from the Ming encyclopedia, *Yung-lo ta-tien* (*op. cit.*) and had them published, along with some of Hsin's prose works, under the title of *Chia-hsüan chi ch'ao-ts'un.* After a more exhaustive search in local gazetteers and rhyming dictionaries, Teng Kuang-ming found in 1939 another eleven poems attributed to Hsin. (For the text of these poems, see PP 45–65.) Except for a few poems written in the "ancient poetry" (*ku-shih*) style, and a dozen or so in the *lü-shih* meter, most of the hundred-odd poems are of the *chüeh-chü* type. Nearly all of them are occasional poems, poems sent to someone else, or poems of humor, including fifteen quatrains mourning the death of a son (who died early) [PP 57–58]. Quite a few of them involve punning, but none possess the poetic quality of his lyrics.

In the classification of "tune patterns," Chinese critics rather arbitrarily decided to call those of under 58 words "small songs" (*hsiao-ling*), those of 59-90 words "middle tunes" (*chung-tiao*), and those of above ninety words "long tunes" (*ch'ang-tiao*). The two *Hua-chien* patterns appearing on this list are Numbers 2 and 4, classifiable respectively as "middle tune" and "small song." Four of the seven on this list of Hsin's most favored patterns are "long tunes."

The longest of *tz'u* patterns, 240 words, with the title of *Ying-t'i-hsü,* does not occur in Hsin's works; the longest pattern he ever used is *Shao-pien* (see Chapter 6, Poems 37 and 38), with 203 words, which is the third longest of all *tz'u* patterns.

2. *Hua-chien chi,* SPPY edition, Preface, p. 1.

3. *Ibid.,* 4/9b.

4. *Ibid.,* 4/9a. It should be noted that Hsin chose to add the word *T'ang* to the original title, possibly to indicate his knowledge of the early origin of this tune as from the T'ang dynasty.

5. This tune is also popularly known as "Hundred-word Song" (*pai-tzu-ling*); see note 1 in this chapter.

6. Actually, one of Hsin's lyrics (Poem 2) was mentioned by a contemporary as having been suspected of containing some plagiarism. Yüeh K'o wrote in the same entry in *T'ing-shih* cited earlier (see note 13, Chapter 3) that in that year (1205) he had seen an "old edition" of the collected lyrics of K'ang Po-k'o (courtesy-name of K'ang Yü-chih,

fl. 1131), under the title of *Shun-an yüeh-fu* (now lost), which included a lyric written to the tune of "Full River Red" and containing several lines identical with Hsin's lines. The lines cited by Yüeh included the last ten words in Stanza 1 from Hsin's lyric, an entire couplet (lines 18–19) in Stanza 2, and the last three lines (with one word altered) of Stanza 2. (For this fragment of K'ang's poem, see CST, pp. 1302–3.) However, Yüeh, who had access to the entire poem (the alleged original) went on to say that, upon examining the whole poem, he discovered "an obvious incongruity of style between these lines and the rest of the poem." This admission seems to indicate that Yüeh had already suspected the text in question to be corrupt.

Poem 2, though the date of composition is said to be undetermined according to Teng Kuang-ming, has to be an early work of Hsin's since it appeared in the "B" *chüan* of the four-*chüan* edition; it is dated as early as 1174, based on stylistic analysis, by Cheng Ch'ien (*Chia-hsüan tz'u chiao-chu*, p. 11). K'ang, on the other hand, is the least likely person either to have written these lines or to have won the admiration of Hsin. Known as one of the chief supporters of Ch'in Kuei, the architect of the appeasement policy, he was exiled after 1155; but, before banishment, he won a small reputation as a kind of "court lyricist" in the court of Emperor Kao-tsung. The thirty-eight poems of his included in the CST, collected from various sources by a modern editor, include four entitled "Boudoir Thoughts," one entitled "On the Birthday of the Prime Minister," one other written on the subject of a royal outing, three others written "at Imperial Request" (*ying-chih*) on festival days, besides three other lyrics that in another anthology had been wrongly attributed to Kao-tsung himself. In both content and style, these lyrics bear no resemblance whatsoever to the lines in question. It is also very common, in the printing of the individual works of *tz'u* poets, to make mistaken attributions of authorship; it is conceivable that these lines of Hsin's could have been mistakenly included in that lost volume of *Shun-an yüeh-fu*.

7. Line 1 is taken from a poem in the *Chiu-pien* (The Nine Arguments) in *Ch'u Tzu* (SPPY edition, 8/4a). The poem is traditionally ascribed to Sung Yü (*fl.* 298 B.C.–265 B.C.), a follower of Ch'ü Yüan. The translation by David Hawkes of lines 3–4 of this poem reads: "Sad and lorn! as when on journey far one climbs a hill and looks down on the water to speed a returning friend" (Hawkes, p. 92).

Line 2 is the line 13 of "Shao Ssu-ming" (The Lesser Master of Fate), the sixth poem in the cycle known as *Chiu-ko* (The Nine Songs) in *Ch'u Tz'u* (2/15a). Cf. Hawkes, p. 41, where this line is translated as "No sorrow is greater than the parting of the living."

Line 3 is taken from the poem "On Ascending the Height at Ch'i-an on the Ninth," CTS, p. 3146. Line 4 is identical with a line from a poem (*shih*) by Su Shih; see *Tung-p'o chi*, SPPY ed., 5/5a. But these three words: *Ku-jen fei* could have come from some other sources. For example, a lyric by Hsin's philosopher-friend, Chu Hsi, also has a line: *Hsi-jen fei* (CST, p. 1675), which reads *ku-jen fei* in the *Tz'u-tsung* (SPPY ed., 14/3b), the general anthology compiled by Chu I-tsun (1629–1709).

Line 5 is the last line of an "ancient-style" poem by Li Ch'iao, entitled "The Ballad of Feng-yin"; see CTS, p. 408.

8. *Ching-chieh hsien-sheng chi*, SPPY edition, 1/1a–2a. The word *t'ing* means "to stop, or pause," translated as "lingering" by Chang and Sinclair (*The Poems of T'ao Ch'ien*, p. 11). This poem of T'ao Ch'ien's was also much admired by Su Shih; cf. Su's "Ho T'ing-yün" poem, *Tung-p'o hsü-chi*, 3/2b. But *ho* (to harmonize merely calls for the echoing of sentiments and the use of some words from the original; whereas in Poem 24, except for the last three lines, all the words are taken from either the preface or the poem by T'ao, with the addition of a dozen extra words by Hsin Ch'i-chi.

9. For the date of Li Ch'ing-chao's death, I follow Huang Sheng-chang, "Chao Ming-ch'eng, Li Ch'ing-chao fu-fu nien-p'u," *Li Ch'ing-chao chi* (Shanghai, 1962), pp. 112-167.

10. *Tz'u-tsung*, 25/1b.

11. The transmission of the text of Li Ch'ing-chao's lyrics has an obscure history. The earliest bibliography to mention her works in print is Ch'ao Kung-wu's *Chün-chai tu-shu chih* (see *Li Ch'ing-chao chi*, p. 220); but a bibliography of slightly later date, Ch'en Chen-sun's (*fl.*, 1234–36) *Chih-chai shu-lü chieh-t'i*, lists her works as consisting of one *chüan* of lyrics and five *chüan* of "other editions" (*pieh-pen*). TSCC reprint, p. 588.

12. Liu Wu-chi, *An Introduction to Chinese Literature* (Bloomington, 1966), p. 116.

13. See K. Y. Hsü, "The Poems of Li Ch'ing-chao (1094–1141)." *PMLA*, LXXVII (1962), 521–28.

14. CST, p. 928 ("Feng-huang t'ai-shang i-ch'ui-hsiao").

15. CST, p. 929.

16. The last line of this famous lyric by Li Yü, the last ruler of Southern T'ang kingdom, reads: *pieh-shih i-pan tz'u-wei tsai hsin-t'ou*, which describes the "grief of separation" of the previous line. In a close paraphrase, this line means: "You could never expect it, but it has a kind of flavor of its own felt by the heart." This line has been remarkably well translated as "With a flavor all its own for the heart," by Robert Kotewall and Norman L. Smith, *The Penguin Book of Chinese Verse*, p. 36. But cf. another version of the same line in Alan Ayling and

Duncan Mackintosh, *A Collection of Chinese Lyrics* (London, 1965), p. 51: "It leaves the heart with a stain, the bruise of its blow."

17. CST, p. 928 ("I-chien-mei").

18. Another difficult line to translate because of colloquialisms, but it has been accurately translated as "It has just left the eyebrows/ When once again it enters the heart" (Liu Wu-chi, *op. cit.*, p. 116).

19. *Tu Shao-ling chi hsiang-chu,* 17/59.

20. Ting, p. 1427 ("Jo-yeh hsi" poem). The first line of Wang Chi's couplet must be one of Hsin's favorite passages. In the title of another poem (AL 299), Hsin tells how he came to write that poem, as follows: "While drinking with some guests at Gourd Spring, one of the guests asked whether the noise of waterfalls was noisy or quiet. I was too drunk to find a reply to the question. Someone answered by quoting 'ch'an sao lin yü ching,' and I found that excellent. The next day I wrote this poem to compliment my friend."

21. *Ts'ao-t'ang shih-yü,* SPPY edition, 1/9a.

22. *Nan-T'ang erh-chu tz'u hui-ch'ien,* ed. T'ang Kuei-chang (Shanghai, 1936), 2 b.

23. Ma Ling, *Nan-Tang shu* (TSCC edition), p. 140.

24. CST, p. 225.

25. This line could mean, "Laughing and singing, people came and went." Here Hsin combines the colloquial *ti* with a reduplicative formed of the word *yin* (lit., "to hum verse"). The use of reduplicatives is a celebrated feature of Li Ch'ing-chao's style; cf. the first line of her poem "To the Tune-title of *Sheng-sheng-man*" (which, incidentally, is the same pattern used by Hsin to write his imitation of T'ao Ch'ien, Poem 24 of this chapter)—which reads: *hsün-hsün, mi-mi,/ leng-leng ch'ing-ch'ing,/ ch'i-ch'i ts'an-ts'an ch'i-ch'i,* translated by Hsü (*op. cit.*, p. 526) as "Search and search, look and look again,/ Lonely,/ Chilly, and dreary." Hsin makes several attempts, though none successfully, at imitation. See two lines about plum-blossoms from another lyric [AL 374], which reads: *shou-ling-ling-ti t'ien-ran pai,/ leng ch'ing-ch'ing-ti hsü-to hsiang,* or "Thin and austere—yet naturally fair;/ Cold and lone: and yet so full of fragrance."

The word in the first set of the two reduplicatives is actually an allusion to a line from a rhyme-prose composition by Pao Chao (*ca.* 421–465) describing the frost of autumn: *ling-ling shuang-ch'i* (*Wen-hsüan*; 11/8a). Originally a noun, meaning 'the roof-ridge of a palace," *ling* does occur in a reduplicative to mean "austere-looking," suggestive of authority. The poet's best friend, Ch'en Liang, for instance, happens to use this very word to describe the looks of Hsin, in an "Inscription Written for the Portrait of Chia-hsüan" (NP, p. 148). Its use in this line, therefore, in combination with vernacular expressions, is the more striking.

26. The particle *hsi* (transcribed in its modern pronunciation since its ancient pronunciation cannot be determined) has been identified by Hawkes as "a carrier-sound" and is said to resemble in its function "tra-la" or "fa-la" of ballad poetry (Hawkes, p. 5).

27. Chu Ch'eng-chüeh (Ming dynasty), *Ts'un-yü-t'ang shih-hua,* 12/6; in *Li-tai shih-hua* (Taipei: I-wen, 1956), p. 510.

28. *Lin-ch'uan chi,* SPPY edition, 29/8b.

29. "Departure," *Collected Poems of Thomas Hardy* (New York: Macmillan, 1946), p. 28.

30. *Shuo-wen chieh-tzu-chu* (Taipei: I-wen, 1965), p. 619.

31. Han Yü, "Lung-li" (Officers of Lung) poem, *Ch'ang-li hsien-sheng chi,* SPPY edition, 6/6a. Han Yü's line reads: *te-wu shih ch'i-chien,* or "Are there none who behave like a louse among them?"

32. T. S. Eliot, "Tradition and Individual Talent," *Selected Essays, 1917-1932* (New York: Harcourt, Brace, 1932), p. 4.

33. *Ibid.*

34. *Ibid.,* p. 6.

Chapter Six

1. Cleanth Brooks, *The Language of Poetry* (New York: Russell & Russell, 1960), p. 40.

2. "Wan-ko Shih," *Ching-chieh hsien-sheng chi,* SPPY edition, 4/17b.

3. James R. Hightower, "T'ao Ch'ien's 'Drinking Wine' Poems," *Wen-lin: Studies in the Chinese Humanities,* ed. Chow Tse-tsung (Madison: The University of Wisconsin Press, 1968), p. 23. (The title of the poem is given as "Bearers' Song.")

4. James J. Y. Liu, *The Art of Chinese Poetry,* p. 99.

5. *Tao Teh Ching,* trans. John C. H. Wu (New York: St. John's University Press, 1961), p. 29.

6. *Ibid.,* p. 63.

7. See Introduction by Burton Watson to his translation of *The Complete Works of Chuang Tzu* (New York, 1928), p. 8; cited hereafter as Watson. Also cf. pp. 7–9 for a discussion of the authorship of the *Chuang-tzu* and its relationship to *Tao-te-ching.* In China, philosophical Taoism is alternatively known as the "philosophy of Lao Chuang."

8. Watson, p. 43. P'eng-tsu is "the Chinese Methuselah"; for this paradox, cf. Sir Thomas Browne's "we live with death, and die not in a moment. How many pulses made up the life of Methuselah. . . ." (*Hydriotaphia: Urn-Burial,* Chapter V).

9. See Ch'en, *op. cit.,* pp. 161–67; 220–30. Ch'en's tabulation shows eighty-nine allusions to the *Chuang-tzu,* as against thirty-three to *The Analects* of Confucius, seventeen to the *Book of Mencius,* twenty to all the Buddhist scriptures—in addition to four other allusions to the *Tao-te-*

ching and twenty-five others to the writings of Lieh Tzu, another Taoist philosopher. Ch'en's tabulation, however, is not complete: an allusion to the "Tze-yang" chapter of the *Chuang-tzu*, for instance, is not accounted for (see line 1 of Poem 37).

10. Hightower, *op. cit.; Wen-lin*, p. 12.

11. *Chia-hsüan ch'ang-tuan chü*, Peking photolithographic reprint edition (1959) of the 1299 edition, 7/14a.

12. *Chia-hsüan tz'u*, "B" (*ping*) *chüan*, 16b–17a.

13. This omission has not been noted in Teng Kuang-ming's text (AL 382), which does record, however, the three other textual variants.

In addition to the general elegiac tone of lines 8–10, and the allusion to Yang Hsiung, there are at least two other internal evidences supporting the argument that this poem was an elegy on the death of Chu Hsi: (1) the reference to the "season of rain," since Chu died on the ninth day of the third month in the year of *keng-shen*, or 1200, which falls within the rainy season in the southeastern part of China (cf. Wang Mou-hung, *Chu-tzu nien-p'u*, 2 vols., II, 226); and (2) the similarity of wording between the last two lines of this poem and the four-line fragment of a "requiem" (*chi-wen*) written by Hsin on the death of Chu Hsi, as found in the official biography of Hsin in *Sung shih* (401/6a).

It is the view of Hsia Ching-kuan alone that the title in the twelve-*chüan* edition is "of an unaccountable origin" (AL 581). His view is already refuted by Teng (AL 589), who also accepts this poem as an elegy on the death of Chu Hsi. Teng identifies as an allusion to Tu Fu the last two lines of Hsin's poem. It may make his argument even more cogent if we examine these two lines. The lines are from a quatrain, entitled "Six *chüeh-chü* Poems Written in Jest, Number 2" ("Hsi-wei liu chüeh-chü," *Tu Shao-ling chi hsiang-chu*, 11/54), which contains Tu Fu's thoughts on the fate of the "four young talented poets of the early T'ang": Wang Po, Yang Chiung, Lu Chao-lin, and Lo Ping-wang. It is also a poem of poetic criticism since, in the first line of the poem, Tu ranked the four poets as "Yang, Wang, Lu, Lo," contrary to the contemporary reputation of the poets which ranked Yang second to Wang. Tu Fu's two lines read: "For you fellows, both body and fame have now been annihilated;/ And yet, relentlessly, the river for ten thousand ages [*wan-ku*] flows on." Further, the antithesis between "body" (*sheng*) and "fame" (*ming*) contains an allusion to the *Tao-te-ching* (Chapter 44): "As for your name and your body, which is the dearer?" (Wu, *op. cit.*, p. 63).

This note is being offered to establish the credibility of the title in the later edition as well as to throw further light on Hsin's use of allusions.

14. Watson, p. 302.

15. Teng (NP 6) gives six names: Fei-ch'ing, Ch'ing-ch'ing, Hsiang-

hsiang (the last, however, occurs only as a name in a lyric and is not identified as a concubine or a "waiting-maid," AL 86), T'ien-t'ien, Ch'ien-ch'ien, and Cheng-cheng. See AL 316–17 for poems written about "Ah-ch'ien."

16. *Ch'ing-po pieh-chih,* by Chou Hui [Shan ?] (*fl.* 1126), said to be a son of the lyric poet Chou Pang-yen, is the only source for this story and for the text of this lyric. In recounting the story, Chou's bibliographic note also says that "this poem because of its jocular tone had been left out of the collected works which Chia-hsüan had edited" (AL 191–92), probably referring to the first volume of the four-*chüan* edition.

17. This term, along with the term "pseudological debate," is used by Watson (p. 5) in his analysis of Chuang Tzu's style.

18. In a triolet, as in the "Rose-Leaves" cycle, the first line is repeated as the fourth and seventh lines, while the second line is repeated as the eighth line in each stanza. Cf. "A Kiss":

> Rose kissed me to-day.
> Will she kiss me to-morrow?
> Let it be as it may,
> Rose kissed me to-day,
> But the pleasure gives way
> To a savour of sorrow;—
> Rose kissed me to-day,—
> *Will* she kiss me to-morrow?

(*Complete Poetical Works of Henry Austin Dobson,* Alban Dobson, ed. [London: Oxford University Press, 1923], p. 323.)

19. Hawkes, *op. cit.,* p. 47.
20. *Ibid.,* p. 51
21. *Li T'ai-po ch'üan-chi,* SPPY edition, 23/2b.
22. Liu Wu-chi, *op. cit.,* p. 111 (modified).
23. Watson, p. 284.
24. *Ibid.,* pp. 29–30.
25. *Ibid.,* p. 175.
26. AL 399 ("To the Tune of *Pu-suan-tzu*").
27. Watson, pp. 183–84.
28. *Ibid.,* pp. 101–2.
29. *Ibid.,* pp. 210–11.
30. *Ibid.,* p. 188–89.
31. *Chĭng-chieh hsien-sheng chi,* SPPY edition, 5/8a.
32. *The Analects of Confucius,* trans. Arthur Waley, pp. 111–12.
33. David Jones, Preface, *The Anathémata,* pp. 34–35.
34. *Ibid.,* p. 35.
35. *Ibid.*

Notes to the Poems

POEM 1

line 3, "Eight-hundred-*li* Ox": An allusion to a story found under the topic of "Extravagances" (*chüan* 30) in a famous fifth-century collection of anecdotes by Liu I-ch'ing (403–44) entitled *Shih-shuo hsin-yü* [SSHY]. The story concerns a wager between a noted archer, who also owned a rare ox named "Eight-hundred-*li* Beast [*po*]," and his friend who, professing to be less skilled in archery, wagered a huge sum of money against the ox if he should miss the target in a match. The friend was first to shoot, and, after he had hit the mark, he nonchalantly said, "Fetch me the heart of the animal" (p. 219).

line 4, "fifty-string zithers": An allusion to the "Ornamented Zither" in the poetry of Li Shang-yin (813–58). See James J. Y. Liu, *The Poetry of Li Shang-yin* (Chicago: University of Chicago Press, 1969), pp. 51–57.

line 6, "horse . . . of Liu": The text reads: *Ti-lu*, the name of a stallion owned by Liu Pei, the founder of the Shu kingdom during the Three Kingdoms period.

POEM 2

line 1, "Guest of Hsin-feng": Alluding to the story of Ma Chou (601–48), who was so poor that he was once ignored by the proprietor of an inn at Hsin-feng, where he was staying. Later, in the capital of Ch'ang-an, he stayed in the home of a friend who was a military man. And, through this friend who came to rely upon him for opinions on state affairs, he was brought to the attention of the emperor and was given official posts. See HTS 98/4a; CTS (Liu) 74/4a–4b.

line 2, "coat . . . threadbare": Alluding to the story of Su Ch'in of the Warring States period who had failed in ten attempts to win the support of the king of Ch'in. Consequently, he is said to have experienced great poverty "when his hundred catties of gold had been exhausted and his coat of black sable fur became threadbare" (CKT 3/4a).

line 4, "Tapping . . . sword": Alluding to the story of Feng Hsüan (Huan) of the Warring States period, a skilled "persuader" who, before his discovery by his master, Prince Meng-ch'ang, resorted to numerous stratagems to attract attention, including tapping on his sword. See *Chan-kuo ts'e* [CKT], 4/36b–39a. The name of "Blue Snake" (*ch'ing-she*) in the next line belongs to an ancient sword.

line 11, "land . . . sinking": Alluding to the story of Tung-fang Shuo (161–*ca.* 87 B.C.) a scholar-humorist known also for his unorthodox behavior. When his son, who was also an officer in the court, told him that he was being called "the mad man," he replied that he was only escaping from the world by being in court, unlike the ancient worthies who went to live in the mountains. One day, while he was drunk, he sat on the ground and sang a short song, the first two lines read: *lu-ch'en yü-shu,/ pi-shih Chin-ma Men* ("The land is sinking in vulgarity,/ And I escape from the world at the Gate of Golden Horse"), referring to the gate of the palace where officers alight. See *Shih chi,* p. 3205.

line 16, "the Beautiful One": The text reads: *yü-jen,* a conventional phrase for a woman, possibly referring to a singsong girl at the banquet (according to Hu Yün-i, *Sung tz'u-hsüan,* p. 307).

line 18, "tassels of office": Alluding to the story of Chung Chün (140–113 B.C.), who, in the midst of peace talks with the kingdom of Nan-yüeh (corresponding to the territory of North Vietnam), pleaded with the emperor to be given "long tassels" (*ch'ang-yin*) so that he could "tie up" (*chi*) the king of Nan-yüeh and deliver him to the palace (*Han shu,* 64-*hsia*/8a–8b).

line 19, "sword . . . calf": Alluding to the story of Magistrate Kung Sui, who, in a year of poor harvest, persuaded people to attend to agricultural pursuits and to sell their swords for calves (*Han shu,* 89/10a–12b).

line 21, "Scholar Chia . . . Changsha": The text reads: *Chia Changsha,* referring to Chia I (201–169 B.C.), a brilliant literary genius during Han Wu-ti's reign, who died in exile as Tutor of the Prince of Changsha.

POEM 3

lines 1–2, "autumn wind . . . gently": For "gently" the text reads: *ni-ni,* both the phraseology and the idea derived from four lines from the poem "The Lady of Hsiang" in the *Nine Songs,* translated by David Hawkes as follows: "The Child of God, presiding the northern bank/ Turns on me her eyes that are dark with longing./ Gently the wind of autumn whispers;/ On the waves of the Tung-t'ing Lake the leaves falling" (Hawkes, p. 38).

lines 4–5, "rivers and mountains . . . indifferent": This statement is derived from one of the anecdotes in SSHY. The story (*chüan* 2) is as follows: After the fall of the Western Chin dynasty, those who had crossed the River would gather at the New Pavilion when the weather was good, drinking and feasting. One day, Chou I (269–322) sighed and said, "The scenery is the same, and yet the mountains and rivers do look different"; and all present looked at each other and wept. Only Prime Minister Wang Tao (267–330) angrily retorted, "It is our duty to do our best for the royal family and recover the Central Plains; we cannot just face each other like the prisoners of Ch'u [who cannot forget their native tunes]" (SHHY, p. 22).

The group, no doubt, would include Wang Yen (Wang I-fu, 255–311)—an attribution based upon a remark made by Huan Wen (312–73) that "Wang I-fu and company could not be said to bear no responsibility" for the kingdom's fall (CSCC 98/26a). Wang Yen was a first cousin of Wang Jung, who was one of the "Seven Sages of the Bamboo Grove"; and Wang Yen himself is said to have been extremely handsome and a good conversationalist and expert on the "Mystic Talk" (hsüan-yen) based on the teachings of Lao Tzu and Chuang Tzu (CSCC 43/20b–30a). Hsin, in several of his poems, refers to this group of "Pure Talk" philosophers with contempt.

line 6, "He . . . retire": Paraphrasing a quotation attributed to Ts'ai Che of the Warring States period (CKT, 3/70b).

line 7, "Round Fan": Alluding to the "Song of Lament" (Yüan-ko-hsing) by Lady Pan (Pan Chieh-yü), an Imperial concubine during Han Ch'eng-ti's reign (32–8 B.C.). In the song (Ting, p. 102), the author compares her fate to that of a piece of white silk, cut and made into a round fan, and intimates her fear that the fan would be abandoned and put away at the approach of the autumn season.

line 12, "Wu-ti": The text reads: Mao-ling, the place where Han Wu-ti was buried. For the text of his "Autumn Wind" poem, see Ting, p. 47.

line 19, "watercress . . . sea-perch": Alluding to the story of Chang Han (Chang Chi-yin, ca. 258–319) told in chüan 7 of SSHY (p. 97). While serving as an official in Lo-yang, Chang was reminded one day, when the autumn wind started blowing, of the delicacies of his native place in Kiangsu: the sea-perch (lu) just in season and edible water plants known as shun-ts'ai (Brasenia schreberi) and ku-ts'ai, the former usually made into a soup. And he immediately resigned his office and left for home, saying "In life, one's noblest aim is to please oneself: why should one be tied down by a job thousands of miles from home, in pursuit of fame and titles?"

line 22, "the Grand Historian": Ssu-ma Ch'ien, the Grand Historian, besides being one of Hsin's favorite authors, is said to have visited K'uai-chi in search of the "caves of Emperor Yü"; his Shih chi also contains a chapter on the life of Ssu-ma Hsiang-ju.

POEM 4

line 1, "General Li": The story of Li Kuang (*d*. 119 B.C.) is told in *chüan* 109 of *Shih chi* (pp. 2867–78). In one episode, he is said to have been captured alive by the Hsiung-nu tribe, or the Huns. While he was being carried on the back of two horses, he pretended to be dead, and, suddenly, noticing a soldier riding on a fine horse nearby, he jumped on the horse and also took the soldier's bow. So equipped, he galloped for several scores of *li* to rejoin his troop (*Shih chi*, pp. 2870–71).

line 3, "cousin Ts'ai": *Ibid.*, pp. 2873–74.

POEM 5

lines 1–4, "Former General . . . him": The story referred to is told in *Shih chi* (p. 2871) as follows: While he was living in retirement in the South Mountains of Lan-t'ien district, Li returned home one night after a hunting trip and some drinking; and he was stopped by a drunken officer of Pa-ling Pavilion who demanded to know his identity. One of Li Kuang's party replied, "This is the Former General Li," to which the officer retorted, "Even the present generals [i.e., those in active service] are not allowed to travel at night; how can a Former General?" Later, after Li had been reappointed as magistrate, he had this drunken officer executed.

line 5, "taciturn . . . millions": The text reads: *t'ao-li wu-yen* (lit., "Peach and plum trees are without speech"), referring to a proverb quoted by Ssu-ma Ch'ien in the Eulogy section of the biography of Li Kuang (*Shih chi*, p. 2878). The passage reads: "General Li was taciturn by nature, but on the day of his death people throughout the empire mourned his death, whether they knew him or not. Just as the proverb says, 'Peach and plum trees do not speak, but people beat a path under these trees [when the fruits are ripe]'; this is to use a trivial remark to illustrate his greatness."

lines 6–7, "He . . . bow-string": Li Kuang is known for his courage and physical strength. In the episode referred to here, Li is said to have shot, during a hunting trip, at a boulder which was hidden by tall grass and was mistaken by him as a tiger. The arrow pierced the rock. Upon being informed of the error, he tried again to aim his arrow at the boulder, but his arrow could never again pierce the rock.

line 10, "Tu . . . River": Tu Fu, in one of his "Meandering River" (*Ch'ü-chiang*) poems (*Tu Shao-ling chi hsiang-chu*, 2/77), probably written in 752, talked about his own fate by referring to this episode of Li Kuang's life. Hsin used a number of phrases from this poem which I have translated as follows:

I reckon that for this life of mine I cannot blame Heaven;
At the bend of Tu Village, I am lucky to have fields of mulberry
 and hemp.
I should move on purpose, to live by the side of South Mountain;
Wearing a short cloak and on a single horse, I shall keep company
 with Li Kuang,
And watch the shooting of fierce tigers to end my waning years.

line 13, "See . . . tears": This line reads: *K'an feng-liu k'ang-k'ai* (lit.,
"See this man of great charm and character lamenting and sighing").
The problem of translating these two compounds has been discussed
in Chapter 3.

POEM 6

Title: for "cousin" the text reads "Twelfth Younger Brother," referring
to the poet's younger first cousin. The title of the poem also includes
the following: *"T'i-chüeh* and *tu-chüan* are really two kinds of bird.
The difference between them appears in the Supplementary Annotation of *Li Sao."* (See note immediately below.)
lines 1–5, "cuckoo": In lines 1, 3, and 4 of the original, actually three
different names of birds are used: respectively, *t'i-chüeh, che-ku,*
and *tu-chüan,* all referring to a species of birds identified either as
Francolinus chinesis (*che-ku*) or as *Cuculous poliocephalus* (*tu-
chüan*). The latter sings at equinox, and its singing marks the end
of spring. The last-mentioned two subspecies have other common
names in Chinese such as *tzu-kuei, tu-yü,* etc. The oldest of the
three names is *t'i-chüeh,* which appears in *Li Sao* (line 151); the
passage is translated by Hawkes as follows: "Beware lest the shrike
sound his note in the equinox,/ Causing all the flowers to lose
their fine fragrance" (Hawkes, p. 32). Besides shrike, the name of
this species has also been rendered into English as cuckoo, night-
jar, goatsucker, or partridge. Also cf. James J. Y. Liu, *The Poetry
of Li Shang-yin,* p. 45.
line 9, "tune . . . border": *P'i-p'a,* or "balloon-guitar," is traditionally
associated with the story of Wang Chao-chün (also Wang Ch'iang),
a palace attendant during the reign of Han Yüan-ti (*r.* 48–32
B.C.), who was so proud of her beauty that she refused to bribe the
court painter to paint her more beautiful than she was. Thus ne-
glected by the emperor, she was later given in marriage to a Hun
chieftain, and the emperor discovered her beauty only when she
came to bid farewell. The earliest poem to mention her singing to
the tune of the *p'i-p'a* as she left China appears in the preface of

"Wang Chao-chün Tz'u," written by Shih Ts'ung (249–300); cf. Ting, pp. 532–33.

line 10, "kingfisher carriage": For "Palace" the text reads: *Ch'ang-men,* alluding to the "Ch'ang-men Fu" (A Rhyme-prose Composition on the Long-gate [Palace]), attributed to Ssu-ma Hsiang-ju and said to have been commissioned by Empress Ch'en while she was out of favor with Han Wu-ti (*r.* 140–86 B.C.). The composition, describing the grief of a rejected woman, so moved the emperor that Empress Ch'en won back her favor. Other commentators believe that "Ch'ang-men" merely refers to a palace in Han times and that this line continues the allusion to the Wang Chao-chün story (Hu Yün-i, *Sung Tz'u-hsüan,* p. 304).

lines 11–12, "girl . . . away": For "girl" the text reads: *Yen-yen,* a reduplicative formed of the word meaning "swallow," alluding to the first line of a poem in the *Book of Poetry* ("The Airs of P'ei," No. 3; Arthur Waley, *The Book of Songs,* No. 114). According to the Commentary, which Hsin must have followed, the poem is a song of farewell written by Duke Chuang of Wei and lamenting the departure of his concubine with the name of Yen-yen.

lines 13–15, "A general . . . friend": Alluding to the story of General Li Ling (*d.* 74 B.C.), grandson of Li Kuang, who surrendered to the Huns after being overwhelmed and having exhausted his supply of arrows. This detail is mentioned in Ssu-ma Ch'ien's letter to Jen An ("Pao Jen Shao-ch'ing shu"), *Wen-hsüan,* 41/1a–5a; English translation by James R. Hightower, in *Anthology of Chinese Literature,* ed. Cyril Birch (New York: Grove Press, 1965), pp. 95–102. Li Ling is also known as the bosom friend of Su Wu (*ca.* 143–60 B.C.), who, after spending nineteen years in captivity by the Huns, returned to Han China. Three poems with the title of "Sent to Su Wu," attributed to Li Ling, contain the two lines alluded to here: "Holding your hands and mounting the river's bridge,/ A wanderer at dusk is full of homeless thoughts" (Ting, p. 76).

lines 16–19, "On the bank . . . song": Alluding to the story of Ching K'o, hired by the prince of Yen to assassinate the First Emperor of Ch'in. At a farewell banquet given in his honor just before he left on his mission, all the guests wore white, which was the color of mourning in China. And to the accompaniment of a five-stringed lute, Ching K'o sang these words: "The wind wails and soughs, and *I* River is cold;/ A brave warrior, once left, will never return" (*Shih chi,* p. 2534).

POEM 7

Title: Shih Cheng-chih, whose courtesy-name was Chih-tao, served as the magistrate of Chien-k'ang in 1167. Convinced of the strategic importance of Chien-k'ang, Shih had attempted to persuade Emperor Kao-tsung to make it, instead of Lin-an, the capital.

line 4, "tiger's . . . coil": The text reads: *hu-chü lung-pang* (lit., "to stand there like a tiger and to coil like a dragon"), said of the city of Nanking and its surrounding hills, the Chung Mountains. This is a quotation attributed to Chu-ke Liang, the strategist of the Shu kingdom, who is said to have praised the city, then the capital of Wu, in these words (Quoted in AL, p. 11).

line 10, "sound . . . grove": Alluding to a line from a lyric by Huang T'ing-chien (1045–1105), to the tune of "The Charm of Nien-nu," written on the subject "Awaiting the moon's arrival on the seventeenth day of the eighth month, in the company of several nephews and a famous flutist" (CST, p. 385).

lines 11–15, "Hsieh An": The text reads: *An-shih,* the courtesy-name of Hsieh An, a man known for his elegance of manners and for his sagacity. A story about his composure is told as follows: In 383, the huge army of Fu Chien, a Tibetan general who had become the ruler of the Earlier Ch'in kingdom, was defeated by his nephew Hsieh Hsüan (343–88) and his younger brother Hsieh Shih (327–88), and the news was brought to him while he was playing chess. He did not allow the message to interrupt his game; and, when the game was over, he remarked, "Our children [*hsiao-erh-pei*] have broken up the rebels" (CSCC 79/10b).

POEM 8

Title: The Pei-ku ("Northern Firmness") Pavilion, situated north of Ching-k'ou (modern Chen-chiang in Kiangsu), overlooks the Yangtze. It was built by Ts'ai Mo (281–356) and later repaired by Hsieh An. Cf. YTCS, p. 1178.

line 3, "King of Wu": The text reads: *Sun Chung-mo,* the courtesy-name of Sun Ch'üan, founder of the Wu kingdom (*r.* 222–52).

line 9, "royal Chi-nu": The nickname of Liu Te-yü (Liu Yü), who later became the founder of the (Southern) Sung kingdom and known as Wu-ti (*r.* 420–22). Before his usurpation, which ended the Chin dynasty, he had lived in Ching-k'ou as a commoner.

line 13, "debacle . . . era": "Yüan-chia" is the reign title of the third ruler of the (Southern) Sung kingdom, known as Wen-ti (*r.* 424–54), who waged frequent disastrous military campaigns against the Northern (Toba) Wei dynasty (386–451). The text for this line reads: *Yüan-chia ts'ao-ts'ao* (lit., "Yüan-chia hastily"), meaning "The plans of the Yüan-chia era so hastily drawn up."

line 14, "vain . . . Lang-chü-hsü": The text of this line reads: *feng*

Lang-chü-hsü (lit., to offer or perform sacrifices at Mount Lang-chü-hsü"). Mount Lang-chü-hsü was a mountain given to the famous general Huo Ch'ü-ping (145–117 B.C.) by Han Wu-ti as a reward for his victory over the Huns (*Shih chi, chüan* 111; p. 2396). But the line actually alludes to a later story of the Sung kingdom: Wang Hsien-mo (*d.* 468) was so eager to engage the enemy, the Northern Wei, that the emperor is said to have remarked, "To listen to Hsien-mo talk makes one wish to sacrifice to Mount Lang-chü-hsü," *Sung shu* (History of the Sung [Kingdom]), 76/5a. In ancient China, emperors or their deputies periodically offered sacrifices to sacred or famous mountains as an act of homage to Heaven.

line 16, "Forty-three years": Cf. Yüeh K'o's memoir, *T'ing-shih,* quoted in Chapter 3, pp. 60–61. This entry is dated the year of *I-ch'ou,* or 1205, when Yüeh mentioned this lyric as among Hsin's new compositions. The events referred to in this line must be Hsin's exploits of 1162.

line 20, "Buddha-fox": "Buddha-fox," or Fo-li, is the pet name of the third emperor of the Northern Wei kingdom, known as T'ai-wu-ti (*r.* 424–51), whose cruelty and boldness made him much feared by the (Southern) Sung kingdom.

lines 22–24, "General . . . rice": Alluding to the story of Lien P'o, a famous general of the third century B.C., in the service of the king of Chao. The king wished to employ him against Ch'in and sent an emissary to find out if he would be too old to serve. Suspecting this design, Lien demonstrated his fitness before his guest by consuming in one meal a peck of rice and ten catties of meat. However, having been bribed by Lien's enemy, the emissary falsified the report to the king upon his return and said, "The general could still eat rice, but during the short time of our conversation he had to go out to urinate three times" (*Shih chi, chüan* 81, pp. 2448–2449).

POEM 10

line 1, "Temple and Court": The text reads: *Chung-ting* (lit., "bell and tripod"), referring to temple bells and the sacrificial vessels used in court ceremony. This metonymy is borrowed from Tu Fu's "Ch'ing-ming" Poem, Number One (*Tu Shao-ling chi hsiang-chu,* 22/29).

POEM 11

line 2, "jeweled box": The text reads *ts'ui-lien,* a conventional epithet for a lady's dressing, or cosmetics, box, which usually had a mirror. When not in use, it was usually closed and the mirror placed face down.

line 3, "staff and shoes": The text reads: *chang-chü* (lit., "staff and sandals"). This alliterative compound is often used as a verb meaning "to stroll"; hence, this line can also be translated as "The Master, unhurried, takes his stroll."

line 5, "sea gulls . . . oath": This alludes to a popular story found in *Lieh-tzu* (SPPY edition, 2/13a) and elsewhere in the philosophical writings of ancient China. According to the story, a boy who played on the seashore, daily enjoying the company of sea gulls, one day reported this to his father. His father then asked him to capture one of the sea gulls on his next trip and bring it home. When he appeared again on the seashore, not a single sea gull would come down to play with him. Also cf. a poem by Wang Wei which alludes to this story: "For what reason should the sea gulls be suspicious of me?" (CTS, p. 712). In this line, however, Hsin combines this story with the words about "alliance" (*meng*) borrowed from *Tso chuan*, "9th Year of Duke Hsi," Legge, *The Chinese Classics*, Vol. V, p. 152.

POEM 12

line 1, "the Capital": The text reads: *Ch'ang-an*, capital of ancient China, occurring always in Hsin's poems as a metonymy for the capital of Sung China.

line 3, "the unflavored among flavors": Alluding to a line from Chapter XXXV of *Tao-te-ching*, which describes "the Great Form" (*hsiang*) of Tao as "insipid and tasteless."

line 4, "the useful . . . useless": Alluding to a story told in the chapter "Shan-mu," or "The Mountain Tree," in the *Chuang-tzu*. According to this story, when the philosopher Chuang Tzu one day saw a flourishing tree too large to be used for timber being spared by a woodcutter, he called the attention of his disciples to the advantage of being "useless." The same evening, when they stopped at a house for the night and the host ordered a goose to be killed for supper, the host asked his servant to kill the goose that could not cackle rather than the one that could. The next morning, when queried by his disciples about the seeming contradiction in his opinion concerning the advantage of being "useless," or "worthless," as conducive to long life, Chuang Tzu replied, "I'd probably take a position halfway between worth and worthlessness." (Translation by Burton Watson, p. 209.)

line 5, "I . . . be myself": Alluding to the story about Huan Wen (312–73) found in *chüan* 9 ("Appraisal of Character") of SSHY. The story is as follows: "Huan Wen, in his youth, enjoyed a reputa-

tion equaled by that of Yin Hao [*d.* 356]; and he constantly enter-
tained the desire of outshining Yin. One day Huan asked Yin, 'How
do you compare with me?' Yin answered, 'I have spent much time
with myself; I would rather be myself' " (p. 130).

line 6, "Why . . . someone else?": Alluding to a story found in *Fa-yen,*
a work modeled after *The Analects* of Confucius by Yang Hsiung.
The story is told about a recluse, named Cheng Tzu-cheng, who
took to farming in order to preserve his integrity, and yet he became
widely known in the capital. At the end of the story, the author
remarked, "Why should he be someone else?" (SPTK edition,
5/5b). This line, consisting of three words: *ch'i-ch'i-ch'ing,* is taken
verbatim by Hsin—as is the previous line from SSHY.

POEM 13

line 5, "Each fleck of white": The text reads: *hsing-hsing* (lit., "star
[upon] star"), an epithet for white hair.

POEM 14

Title: I have translated as "replying to" the word *ho,* which is sometimes
rendered as "harmonizing," referring to the custom of writing a
poem "in reply" to the one sent from a friend (usually by employing
the same rhyme words, but not always).

Chao Pu-yü, whose courtesy-name was Chin-ch'en, earned his
chin-shih degree in 1154 and later retired to Shang-jao. Hsin exchanged many poems with him during his second period of residence
at Shang-jao.

POEM 15

line 1, "autumn's frost": The text reads: *yen-shuang* (lit., "wild-geese
frost"), with *yen* suggestive of the season of autumn when wild
geese fly south.

line 17, "Fairyland": The text reads: *Yao-ch'ih,* or Jasper Pond, the
meeting place between the legendary King Mu of Chou (of tenth
century B.C.) and the Queen Mother of the West, who conferred
immortality upon the emperor. See *Mu-t'ien-tzu chuan,* SPPY
edition, 3/1a–1b.

POEM 16

Title: Supplied by Teng, following *Hua-an tz'u-hsüan;* no title given in
either the four-*chüan* or the twelve-*chüan* edition.

line 8, "lies": For the word *wo* (from the four-*chüan* text), the 1299
edition reads: *k'an;* lit., "to watch (others)."

POEM 19

Title: The word "alone" (*tu*) does not appear in the four-*chüan* edition. "Rain Cliff" has been tentatively identified as the Rain Stone Mountain ("Yü-shih Shan"), which is mentioned in YTCS, 21/5a, as being located fifteen miles southeast of Yung-feng *hsien*.

line 8, *i-ch'ü t'ao-hua-shui:* This line can be translated, more literally, either as "one bend of peach-blossom water" or as "one song of peach-blossom water." My translation assumes that there might have been a pun concealed in the word *ch'ü,* which has two common meanings: "a dramatic song" and "a winding body of water." The last three words make up an ambiguous phrase which is said by one scholar to refer to the reflection in the water of peach trees growing on the banks (Hu Shih, *Tz'u-hsüan* [Shanghai, 1927; Taipei, 1959], p. 233). Another translator prefers to think of the peach blossoms as floating on the water; see Ch'u Ta-kao, *Chinese Lyrics* (Cambridge University Press, 1937), p. 45. The line, incidentally, may be considered as a good illustration of synesthesia in Chinese poetry, since the poet employs in one line three senses: the auditory, the visual, and the olfactory.

POEM 20

Title: This title, missing from both the four-*chüan* and the twelve-*chüan,* is supplied by Wang Chao in the second printing of the twelve-*chüan* text in 1536.

line 8, "cassia tree": According to popular Chinese mythology, a cassia tree grows on the moon.

POEM 21

Title: Instead of *t'i,* or "style," the four-*chüan* edition reads: *chi,* "collection" or "anthology."

line 4, "Hsi-tzu": Referring to a famous beauty of the fifth century B.C., also known as Hsi Shih.

POEM 22

line 1, "wild-plum": Both for four-*chüan* and the twelve-*chüan* editions give the character for "plum," which reads *t'ang,* meaning a tree of the crab-apple or wild-plum variety. In many popular editions and anthologies, this word *t'ang* is changed to another character, also read as *t'ang,* which means "creek." This change is actually an emendation made by Wang Chao in the 1536 reprint of the twelve-*chüan* edition, later followed by Mao Chin. "Petals have fallen on deserted creeks" would be the reading of this line if Wang's emendation were accepted.

line 3, "Ch'ing-ming": The "Ch'ing-ming" ("Bright and Clear") festival usually falls during the first week of April in China, when families often go to the countryside to visit ancestral graves.

POEM 25

Title: In the four-*chüan* edition, the last word of the title (*chin*) is inadvertently left out.

line 2, "quickly over": The text reads: *i-sa-erh chia*, a colloquialism meaning "in a short while." *Erh* follows the twelve-*chüan* edition; *shih* (time) is given in the four-*chüan* edition instead of the more colloquial *erh*.

line 6, "homes": The text reads: *jen-chia*, following the twelve-*chüan* edition, but *jen-chien* (human world) in the four-*chüan* edition.

line 8, "summer": The text reads: *hsia*, which is emended to read *sa* (moment) in the Wang (1536) reprint, followed by the Mao edition.

lines 14–19, "But . . . else?": The text of these lines completely disappears from the 1536 reprint and the Mao edition; instead, the text of an entire poem written to the tune of *Tung-hsien-ko* ("Song of Grotto Fairy") is by mistake incorporated as part of this lyric.

lines 14–15, "sea gulls . . . come": Alluding to the same story in note to line 5 of Poem 11.

POEM 29

line 8, "dog's kennel": Alluding to the story about Chang Hsüan-chih (Chang Wu-hsing) in the twenty-fifth chapter ["Poking Fun" ("P'ai-t'iao")] of SSHY (*chüan* six; p. 198): "Chang Wu-hsing, at eight years of age, lost his teeth. His elders, knowing him to be unusually bright, teased him by saying 'How is it that you had a dog's kennel in your mouth?' Without a moment's hesitation, Chang replied, 'Just so that you people can walk in and out.' "

POEM 30

line 8, "thing within the cup": The text reads: *pei-chung-wu* (which is literally translated here), a humorous term for wine. The entire line is a verbatim borrowing from T'ao Ch'ien's "Scolding My Sons" poem ("Tse tzu," *Ching-chieh hsien-sheng chi*, SPPY edition, 3/27a–27b), in which T'ao, after playfully cataloguing the shortcomings of his five sons, writes, "If my fate, decreed by Heaven, is like this / then let me partake of this thing within the cup."

POEM 36

line 5, "phoenix-birds": The text reads: *luan-feng* (lit., "female and male phoenix").

line 6, "Green Mountain" and "Red Cliff": Referring to Li Po and
Su Shih, respectively. Li Po is the author of a poem "Conversation
in the Mountains" ("Shan-chung wen-ta," *Li T'ai-po ch'üan-chi*,
SPPY edition, 19/2b), which includes the following lines: "You
ask why I nestle in the green mountains./ I laugh but answer not—
my heart is serene" (translation by Liu Wu-chi, *op. cit.*, p. 77).
And Su Shih is the author of the two rhyme-prose compositions on
the "Red Cliff" (see Chapter 1).

line 8, "Big Dipper": The text reads: *Pei-tou* (lit., "the Northern Dipper"), alluding to a line from "The Lord of the East" ("Tung-
chüan") poem in the "Nine Songs" (*Chiu ko*) of *Ch'u Tz'u*, which
reads in Hawkes's translation as "I seize the Dipper to ladle cin-
namon wine" (Hawkes, p. 42).

line 13, "Great Swan, one two": Alluding to two lines from a fragment,
by Chia I, entitled "Sorrow for Troth Betrayed" ("Hsi Shih"). The
lines are included in the *Ch'u Tz'u:* "I caused the great swan to
soar at a single bound. / And we saw every wind and bend of
mountain and river . . . [I caused the great swan to] soar a second
time, / And we looked on the whole world, round heaven and
square earth" (translation by Hawkes, p. 116).

lines 17–19, "eclipse . . . Moon": Alluding to the last lines of the lyric
by Su Shih cited earlier in the chapter, which read in Liu Wu-chi's
translation as "The moon . . . waxes and wanes— / This imperfec-
tion has been since ancient time. / Would that we could live a long
life/ And together share the moonlight a thousand miles away!"
For Su's "moonlight" and Hsin's "Lady of the Moon" in line 19,
the text in both poems reads: *Ch'an-chüan* (originally meaning
"beautiful," but used by both poets to refer to moonlight or moon-
goddess.)

POEM 37

Title: "Ch'iu-shui Kuan," also called "Ch'iu-shui T'ang," is the name
given by the poet to a building in his villa when he was living in
Ch'ien-shan *hsien*. The poem explains the reason for the name.

line 9, "heaven . . . rice": This comparison, also from "Autumn Floods,"
occurs in the speech by the God of the Ocean. Watson's translation
of the passage reads: "Compare the area within the four seas with
all that is between heaven and earth—is it not like one little anthill
in a vast marsh? Compare the Middle Kingdom with the area
within the four seas—is it not like one tiny grain in a great store-
house?" (p. 176).

line 13, "Robber Chih . . . wrong": Alluding to an apocryphal story about Confucius' meeting with a notorious robber named Chih who, however, was the brother of a man of virtue by the name of Liu-hsia Chi. According to the story, told in Chapter 29 of the *Chuang-tzu* (with the title of "Robber Chih"), Confucius went on behalf of Chih's brother, trying to persuade him to change his way of living; instead, he lectured Confucius on the foolishness of Confucian ideals. And Confucius returned to Chih's brother to confess, "I gave myself the burning moxa treatment when I wasn't even sick" (Watson, pp. 323–31).

lines 15–16, "expound . . . ice": Cf. "In Pi-ching *hsien* of Jih-nan, there grow fire-rats whose hair can be woven into cloth which does not burn in fire," recorded in a Sung encyclopaedia, the *T'ai-p'ing yü-lan*, compiled by Li Fan (925–96) under Imperial auspices (820/8a; Chung Hwa reprint, p. 3651). The cloth is known as *huo-wan-pu* (cloth washed-by-fire), or as *huo-shu-pu* (fire-rat-cloth) according to Chou Mi's (1232–1308) *Ch'i-tung yeh-yü* [Words of a Fool from Ch'i-tung], Han-feng-lou edition, 12/9a-9b.

"Ice-silkworm" might have come from an entry in *Shih-i chi* [Records of Forgotten Events] by Wang Chia (*d. ca.* 390) as quoted by Teng (AL 343): "In Mount Yüan-ch'iao, there is a kind of ice-silkworm. Its cocoon forms only after it has been covered up with frost and snow. Over one foot long, it has brilliant colors. Woven into silk, the silk does not dissolve in water; thrown into fire, it will not burn even after one night."

line 20, "Priceless . . . sheepskin": For "priceless" the text reads: *lien-ch'eng* (lit., "contiguous cities," or "of many cities' worth"). This refers to the story of Lin Hsiang-ju, of the Warring States period, whose eloquence was able to restore a priceless jade disc to the Chao kingdom despite the coercion and stratagems practiced upon him by the king of Ch'in, including an offer of fifteen cities. See *Shih chi, chüan* 81; 2439–41.

POEM 38

Title: Even though the tune pattern of "Shao-pien" is found in several variant forms, the form used by Hsin in both Poem 37 and Poem 38 is the same and consists of 203 words. However, in Poem 38 he broke up the sixth line, consisting of eight syllables, into two lines, three syllables and five. In the numbering of the lines for this poem alone, I have arbitrarily decided to keep the line numbers of the first poem in order that I may more conveniently provide a list of the rhyming words (which are the same) used in the two poems, as given below:

Rhyming Word (line no.)	In Poem 37 (translated as)	In Poem 38 (translated as)
3 *li*	li	farm
5 *wei*	feeble	infinite
6 *chi* (lit., "limit")	infinitude (*wu-chi*)	infinite (*wu-chi*)
7 *li*	truth	truth
9 *mi*	rice	rice
12 *chih*	know	inscrutable . . . ?
13 *fei*	wrong	misspent
14 *pei*	sadness	sad
17 *i* (pronounced *yi*)	difference	difference
19 *shih* (lit., "time")	Time	(omitted)
20 *p'i*	-skin	pelt
22 *chih* (lit., "him," or "to go")	(omitted)	headed
25 *shui*	floods	stream
28 *ssu*	banks	banks
29 *hsi*	joy	happy
30 *chi* (lit., "self")	him alone	myself
32 *shih*	gaze	viewed
34 *tzu*	you	you
36 *erh* (a "particle")	after all	after all
39 *i*	that's all (*erh-i*)	dismissed

line 1, "single valley": This line alludes to another passage from the "Autumn Floods" chapter, which reads in Watson's translation as follows: "Prince Mou leaned on his armrest and gave a great sigh, and then he looked up at the sky and laughed, saying 'Haven't you ever heard about the frog in the caved-in well?' He said to the great turtle of the Eastern Sea, 'What fun I have! I come out and hop around the railing of the well, or I go back in and take a rest in the wall where a tile has fallen out. . . . *To have complete command of the water of one whole valley* and to monopolize all the joys of a caved-in well—this is the best there is! Why don't you come some time and see for yourself?' " (Watson, p. 186).

line 5, "Smallest . . . infinite": A quotation from *Chou-i hsi-tz'u* ["Judgments" appended to the "Changes of Chou"], ascribed to King Wen of Chou (*Chou-i chi-chieh,* TSCC edition, p. 378).

lines 7–8, "subtle truth . . . wine": That coarse (lit., *cho* or "turbid," i.e., unrefined and cheap) wine has its own subtlety is an allusion to two lines from Tu Fu: "Coarse wine has its subtle truth:/ Nearly able to console those whose fortunes rise and ebb" (*cho-liao yu miao-li* / *shu yung wei ch'en-fu,* from *Tu Shao-ling chi hsiang-chu,* 4/24).

line 13, "fifty-nine years": Alluding to Chuang Tzu's remark about Confucius, found in the "Imputed Words" chapter from the *Chuang-tzu:* "Chuang Tzu said to Hui Tzu, 'Confucius has been going along for sixty years and he has changed sixty times. What at the beginning he used to call right he has ended up calling wrong. So now there's no telling whether what he calls right at the moment is not in fact what he called *wrong during the past fifty-nine years*'" (Watson, p. 305).

POEM 39

line 5, "Emperor and Thief": The text reads: *Shun* [and] *Chih,* referring, respectively, to the legendary sage-emperor Shun and Robber Chih (see note to line 13 of Poem 37).

lines 5–7, "distinction . . . cock's crow": Paraphrasing a passage from the *Book of Mencius* (13:25) which reads in James Legge's translation as follows: "Mencius said, 'He who rises at cock-crowing, and addresses himself earnestly to virtue, is a disciple of Shun. He who rises at cock-crowing, and earnestly addresses himself to the pursuit of gain, is a disciple of Chih. If you want to know what separates Shun from Chih, it is simply this,—the interval between the thought of gain and the thought of virtue'" (*The Chinese Classics,* 7 vols. [London, 1861], II, 340).

lines 8–10, "sweet-flavored . . . water": For "true friendship" the text reads: *chün-tzu chih chiao* (lit., "the friendship or social intercourse among *chün-tzu*"; i.e., the Confucian "moral" or "superior" man). The passage alludes to an observation in *The Book of Rites* (*Li chi,* SPPY edition, 17/9b–10a), which reads in James Legge's translation as: "Hence the intercourse of a superior man may be compared to water, and that of a small man, to sweet wine. The superior man seems insipid, but he helps to perfection; the small man seems sweet, but he leads to ruin" (*Li Chi: Book of Rites,* 2 vols. [New York: University Books, 1967; reprinted from *The Text of Confucianism,* London, 1885], II, 348).

lines 11–12, "One drop . . . chant": Alluding to a remark made by Prince Ching (Chung-shan Ching-wan) of Han dynasty to the emperor, implying his fear of the power of maligning words: cf. *Han shu* (53/10b).

line 14, "yesterday's . . . verity": See note to line 13 of Poem 38.

line 15, "a cup . . . Joy": For "Serendipity Soup," the text reads: *T'ai-ho t'ang* (lit., "Soup of Great Harmony"). I borrow the word coined by Horace Walpole (meaning "looking for one thing and finding another") to approximate the tone of the Chinese allusion.

"T'ai-ho" Soup is a euphemism for wine coined by the Neo-Confucianist philosopher Shao Yung (Shao Yao-fu, 1011–77) in his autobiography (AL 540); also cf. Shao's poem "T'ai-ho t'ang yin," "A Song About T'ai-ho Soup" (*I-ch'uan chi-jan chi*, SPTK edition, 10/140b). The official biography of Shao Yung in *Sung shih* (427/18b) provides the following information. When Shao first went to Lo-yang to live, he could only afford poor quarters, which he named "the Nest of Peace and Joy" (*An-lo wo*); he also gave himself the style-name of "An-lo hsien-sheng," or Master An-lo. "At mealtime he would drink three or four cups of wine. He would quit as soon as he got slightly inebriated, never reaching the condition of total drunkenness."

Finding List of Titles and Other Translations

30. D:33a	11/9b	4/9b	p. 1945	
31. B:27b–28a	—	—	p. 1902	
32. B:22a	11/11a–11b	4/10a–10b	p. 1920	1933 (p. 78); 1937 (p. 43); 1938 (p. 92); 1940 (p. 368); 1947 (p. 278); 1962 (p. 49); 1964–65 (No. 2; p. 67); 1965 (p. 161); 1966 (p. 122)
33. D:31b	10/11a	4/4b	p. 1944	1937 (p. 42); 1947 (p. 278); 1961 (p. 415); 1964–65 (No. 2; p. 71); 1970 (p. 151)
34. C:21b–22a	10/11b–12a	4/4b	p. 1920	1933 (p. 77); 1937 (p. 48)
35. C:7b	4/16a	—	p. 1912	1966 (p. 123); 1970 (p. 159)
36. D:8a	3/14b–15a	1/18a	p. 1932	
37. C:14a–14b	1/1a–1b	1/1a	p. 1916	
38. C:15a–15b	1/1b–2b	1/1a–1b	p. 1916	
39. —	6/13a	2/16b–17a	p. 1956	

Key to Symbols Used in the Above Finding List

Editions (see Bibliography I A)

(1) Four-*chüan* edition of *Chia-hsüan tz'u* (Fan K'ai, 1188–1203; Han-feng-lou, 1940)

(2) Twelve-*chüan* edition of *Chia-hsüan ch'ang-tuan-chü* (Hsin-chou, 1299; 1959)

(3) Mao edition (composite four-*chüan*), also known as *Chia-hsüan tz'u*

(4) CST, or *Ch'üan Sung Tz'u* [Complete Sung Lyrics], ed. T'ang, 1965

— Not included in that edition

Translations (see Bibliography II C)

1933	Clara Candlin, *The Herald Wind*
1937	Ch'u Ta-kao, *Chinese Lyrics*
1938–39	Teresa Li, in *T'ien-hsia Monthly*
1940	John C. H. Wu, in *T'ien-hsia Monthly*
1947	*The White Pony,* ed. Robert Payne
1949	M. L. Ives, *Chinese Love Songs*
1950	Wong Man, tr., *Poems from the Chinese*
1961	Ch'en Shou-yi, *Chinese Literature: A Historical Introduction*
1962	*A Penguin Book of Chinese Verse*
1964–65	*Chinese Literature* [Monthly] (No. 2 and No. 7, respectively)
1965	*A Collection of Chinese Lyrics*
1966	Liu Wu-chi, *An Introduction to Chinese Literature*
1970	*A Further Collection of Chinese Lyrics*

Selected Bibliography

I. Works in Chinese

A. Editions of Hsin's Works (given in chronological order)

1. *Chia-hsüan tz'u,* 4 *chüan.* 1188–1203; 1917 and 1940. [No copy of the printed edition survived. Text preserved in two hand-copied versions: one version, a Ming text, was found to be riddled with errors; the other got its contents separated. *Chüan* labeled *chia, i,* and *ping* (which we may call "A," "B," and "C") passed into the Chi-ku-ko collection during the Ch'ing dynasty, and were printed by T'ao Hsiang in 1917, in *She-yüan ying-k'an Sung-jen tz'u;* reprinted by Wu Ch'ang-shou in (Ying-k'an) *Sung-Chin-Yüan-Ming-pen tz'u (ssu-shih chung).* The last *chüan (ting,* or "D") was discovered by Chao Wan-li in a second-hand book market in Shanghai in 1939; and the four *chüan* were printed together in a Han-feng-lou edition in 1940.]

2. *Chia-hsüan ch'ang-tuan-chü,* 12 *chüan. Hsin-chou,* 1299; Shanghai, 1959.
[One copy extant, now in Peking Library; a handsome photolithographic reprint, in its original size, issued by Chung Hua Book Company in 1959. The original, a block-print edition, is suspected by Chao Wan-li to have been printed from the calligraphy done by diverse hands in imitation of Hsin Ch'i-chi's handwriting; of which only one page of a manuscript survived, dated 1175, in the form of an "official letter" (*cha-tzu*). See Chao Wan-li, "Lu Yu, Hsin Ch'i-chi shou-kao ho ch'i-t'a chu-tso," *Wen-wu ching-hua,* Number 1 (Peking, 1959), 48–49.]

3. *Chia-hsüan tz'u,* 4 *chüan.* Ed. Wang Chao, 1536; Mao Chin (1598–1659).
[Available in most modern reprints and collections of *tz'u* anthologies, this composite four-*chüan* edition actually follows a text derived from the 1299 twelve-*chüan* edition in content. The text followed by Mao is a "punctuated" (*p'i-tien*) edition of *Chia-hsüan ch'ang-tuan chü,* prepared by Li Lien, printed in 1536 by Wang but no longer extant. Mao removed the punctuation and rearranged the text into four *chüan.*] 1947.

4. *Chia-hsüan shih-wen ch'ao-ts'un.* Ed. Teng Kuang-ming. Shanghai,

[A collection of *shih* and prose works of Hsin's copied down from various sources, enlarged from the collection of a similar nature, the *Chia-hsüan chi ch'ao-ts'un,* compiled by Hsin Ch'i-t'ai in 1582.]

5. *Chia-hsüan tz'u pien-nien ch'ien-chu.* Ed. Teng Kuang-ming. Shanghai, 1957, 1962; Taipei: Chung Hua, n.d.

   [This is the most easily available and the best modern annotated text of Hsin's lyrics. Two other editions, which I have consulted, may be mentioned: Liang Ch'i-ch'ao's *Chia-hsüan tz'u shu-cheng,* 6 *chüan,* Shanghai, 1931, and Cheng Ch'ien's *Chia-hsüan tz'u chiao-chu,* 10 *chüan,* in manuscript.]

B. Chronology, Biography, and Criticism

1. Chronology (*nien-p'u*)

   CH'EN, SSU. *Hsin Chia-hsüan nien-p'u.* In *Liao-hai ts'ung-shu, chi* 6, *ts'e* 10.

   CHENG, CH'IEN. *Hsin Chia-hsüan hsien-sheng nien-p'u.* Peking, 1938.

   LIANG, CH'I-CH'AO. *Hsin Chia-hsüan hsien-sheng nien-p'u.* Shanghai, 1936.

   TENG, KUANG-MING. *Hsin Chia-hsüan nien-p'u.* Shanghai, 1957.

2. Biography

   CHIANG, LIN-CHU. *Hsin Ch'i-chi chuan.* Taipei, 1964.

   CH'IEN, TUNG-FU. *Hsin Ch'i-chi chuan.* Peking, 1955.

   HSIA, CH'ENG-T'AO and YU CHIH-SHUI, *Hsin Ch'i-chi.* Shanghai, 1962.

   HSU, CHIA-JUI. *Hsin Chia-hsüan p'ing-chuan.* Chungking, 1946.

   TENG, KUANG-MING. *Hsin Ch'i-chi (Chia-hsüan) chuan.* Shanghai, 1956.

   TU, CH'ENG-HSIANG. *Hsin Ch'i-chi p'ing-chuan.* Taipei, 1954.

3. Criticism

   CH'EN PIN-JAN. *Hsin Ch'i-chi tz'u chih yen-chiu yü hsin-shang* [Hsin Ch'i-chi's Lyrics: Study and Appreciation]. Hsin-chu, Taiwan, 1966.

   CH'EN, SHU-MEI. *Chia-hsüan tz'u yung-tien feng-lei yen-chiu* [A Classified Study of the Use of Allusions in Chia-hsüan's Lyrics]. M.A. thesis. Taipei: National Taiwan University, 1967.

   CHENG, CH'IEN. *Ts'ung shih tao ch'ü* [From "Lyric" to "Dramatic" Songs]. Taipei, [1961].

   CHIANG, SHANG-HSIEN. *Sung ssu-ta-chia tz'u yen-chiu* [A Study of Four Master Lyric Poets of Sung]. Taipei, 1962.

   HU, YUN-I. *Chung-kuo tz'u shih* [A History of Chinese Lyric Poetry]. Taipei, 1961. [A Reprint.]

   ———. *Sung-tz'u yen-chiu* [A Study of Sung Lyric Poetry]. Shanghai, 1926.

Liu, T'ien-chung. *Hsin Ch'i-chi tz'u chi ch'i sheng-p'ing ssu-hsiang* [Hsin Ch'i-chi's Lyric Poetry and His Thought]. Hong kong, 1969.

T'ang, Kuei-chang (ed.). *Tz'u-hua ts'ung-pien* [Collectanea of Talks on Lyric Poetry], 12 vols. Taipei, 1967. [A Reprint.]

Wang, I. *Tz'u-ch'ü shih* [History of Lyric and Dramatic Poetry], 2 vols. Taipei, 1930.

Wang, Li. *Han-yü shih-lü-hsüeh* [Prosody of Chinese Poetry], Shanghai, 1962.

Wu, Mei. *Tz'u-hsüeh t'ung-lun* [A General History of *tz'u*], Taipei, 1965. [A Reprint.]

II. Publications in English (and French)

A. Bibliography

Davidson, Martha (ed.). *A List of Translations from Chinese into English, French, and German.* Parts I and II. Far Eastern Publications. New Haven: Yale University Press, 1957.

B. Articles on Hsin Ch'i-chi

Lo, Irving Yucheng. "Thirty Lyrics by Hsin Ch'i-chi, 'A Poets' Poet'," *K'uei Hsing,* I (1971). Bloomington: Indiana University Press.

Teng, Kuang-ming. "Hsin Ch'i-chi and His Poetry," *Chinese Literature* (1964; No. 2), pp. 73–78.

C. Translations (and Other Works Containing Hsin's Poetry)

Ayling, Alan and Duncan Mackintosh. *A Collection of Chinese Lyrics.* London: Routledge and Kegan Paul, 1965. Translations are in rhyme and include a total of four of Hsin's poems, two of which, not shown on the Finding List, are also included in Lo's article cited above.

————. *A Further Collection of Chinese Lyrics* (and Other Poems). Nashville, Tennessee: Vanderbilt University Press, 1970. Renditions of twelve additional lyrics by Hsin, five of which (see Finding List) are included in this volume while two others are included in Lo's article on Hsin.

Candlin, Clara M. *The Herald Wind.* Wisdom of the East Series. London: John Murray, 1933. Includes nine of Hsin's poems.

Ch'en, Shou-yi. *Chinese Literature: A Historical Introduction.* New York: Ronald Press. 1961. Pp. 410–18 include seven of Hsin's poems.

CH'U, TA-KAO. *Chinese Lyrics.* Cambridge: University Press, 1937. Includes seven of Hsin's poems.

DAVIS, A. R. (ed.). *The Penguin Book of Chinese Verse.* Tr. by Robert Kotewall and Norman L. Smith. Baltimore: Penguin Books, 1962. Includes one of Hsin's poems.

DEMIÉVILLE, PAUL. *Anthologie de la Poesie chinoise classique.* Paris: Gallimard, 1962. Pp. 405–7 give three of Hsin's poems, including Poem 32 of this book.

IVES, MABEL LORENZ. *Chinese Love Songs.* Upper Montclair, New Jersey: B. L. Hutchinson, 1949. Includes one poem by Hsin.

LI, TERESA. "Poems from the Chinese," *T'ien-hsia Monthly,* VI (1938), 231–54. Includes one of Hsin's poems.

———. "Fifty-six Poems from the Chinese," *T'ien-hsia Monthly,* VII (1939), 61–98. Includes two of Hsin's poems.

LIU, WU-CHI. *An Introduction to Chinese Literature.* Bloomington: Indiana University Press, 1966. Pp. 121–24 include four of Hsin's poems in their entirety and the first stanza of another.

PAYNE, ROBERT. *The White Pony.* New York: John Day, 1947. Includes two of Hsin's poems.

WONG, MAN. *Poems from the Chinese.* Hongkong: Creation Books, 1950. Includes three poems, pp. 113–18.

YANG, HSIEN-YI and GLADYS YANG. "Selections from the Classics: Hsin Ch'i-chi," *Chinese Literature* (1964; No. 2), pp. 65–72; (1965; No. 7), pp. 73–81. Includes a total of nineteen of Hsin's poems.

D. On Other Chinese Poets Frequently Mentioned

ACKER, WILLIAM, tr. *T'ao the Hermit: Sixty Poems by T'ao Ch'ien.* London: Thames & Hudson, 1952.

CHANG, LILY PAO-HU and MARJORIE SINCLAIR, tr. *The Poems of T'ao Ch'ien.* Honolulu: University of Hawaii Press, 1953.

HAWKES, DAVID, tr. *Ch'u Tz'u: The Songs of the South.* London: Oxford University Press, 1959.

HIGHTOWER, JAMES R. "T'ao Ch'ien's 'Drinking Wine' Poems," *Wen-lin: Studies in the Chinese Humanities,* ed. Chow Tse-tsung. Madison: The University of Wisconsin Press, 1968.

HSU, K'AI-YU. "The Poems of Li Ch'ing-chao (1084–1141)," *PMLA,* LXXVII(1962), 521–28.

HU, P'in-ch'ing. *Li Ch'ing-chao.* New York: Twayne Publishers, 1966.

HUNG, WILLIAM. *Tu Fu: China's Greatest Poet.* With *A Supplementary Volume of Notes.* Cambridge: Harvard University Press, 1952.

LIN, YUTANG. *The Gay Genius* [Su Shih]. New York: John Day, 1947.

WATSON, BURTON, tr. *Su Tung-p'o: Selection from a Sung Dynasty Poet.* New York: Columbia University Press, 1965.

E. On Chinese Poetry (and Translation)

ARROWSMITH, WILLIAM and ROGER SHATTUCK (eds.). *The Craft and Context of Translation: A Critical Symposium.* Austin: University of Texas Press, 1961. Contains summaries of several items listed in this bibliography.

BAXTER, G. W. "Metrical Origin of the *Tz'u,*" *Harvard Journal of Asiatic Studies,* XVI (1953), 108–45. [Also appearing in *Studies in Chinese Literature,* John L. Bishop, ed. Harvard-Yenching Institute Studies, XXI. Cambridge: Harvard University Press, 186–224.]

————. *Index to the Imperial Register of Tz'u Prosody.* Harvard-Yenching Institute Studies, XV. Cambridge: Harvard University Press, 1956.

BOODBERG, PETER A. "Cedules from a Berkeley Workshop in Asiatic Philology," *Tsing Hua Journal of Chinese Studies,* New Series VII (August, 1969), 1–39.

BROWER, REUBEN A. (ed.) *On Translation.* Cambridge: Harvard University Press, 1959.

FANG, ACHILLES. "Some Reflections on the Difficulty of Translation," in Brower, pp. 111–33.

FRODSHAM, J. D. "The Origin of Chinese Nature Poetry," *Asia Major,* VIII, Pt. I (1960), 68–103.

————. "Landscape Poetry in China and Europe," *Comparative Literature,* XIX (1967), 193–215.

HAWKES, DAVID. "Chinese Poetry and the English Reader," pp. 90–115 in *The Legacy of China,* Raymond Dawson, ed. London: Oxford University Press, 1964.

LIU, JAMES J. Y. *The Art of Chinese Poetry.* Chicago: University of Chicago Press, 1962.

LUH, C. W. *On Chinese Poetry.* Peiping, 1935.

TEELE, ROY EARL. *Through a Glass Darkly: A Study of English Translations.* Ann Arbor, 1949.

YIP, WAI-LAM. *Ezra Pound's Cathay.* Princeton, New Jersey: Princeton University Press, 1969.

YOSHIKAWA, KOJIRO. *An Introduction to Sung Poetry,* tr. by Burton Watson. Harvard-Yenching Institute Monograph Series, XVII. Cambridge: Harvard University Press, 1967. [Deals exclusively with the *shih* of the Northern Sung dynasty.]

F. On Other Aspects of Society in Sung China

CHAN, WING-TSIT, tr. *Reflections of Things at Hand: The Neo-Confucian Anthology.* Compiled by Chu Hsi and Lü Tsu-ch'ien. New York: Columbia University Press, 1967.

Gernet, Jacques. *Daily Life in China on the Eve of the Mongol Invasion, 1250–1276,* tr. by H. M. Wright. New York: Macmillan, 1962.

KRACKE, E. A., JR. *Civil Service in Early Sung China.* Cambridge: Harvard University Press, 1953.

————. *Translation of Sung Civil Service Titles.* Paris: École pratique des Hautes Études, 1957.

PIAN, RULAN CHAO. *Sonq [Sung] Dynasty Musical Sources and Their Interpretation.* Harvard-Yenching Institute Monograph Series, XVI. Cambridge: Harvard University Press, 1967.

G. Miscellaneous

CONFUCIUS. *The Analects of Confucius,* tr. by Arthur Waley. London: Allen & Unwin, 1938.

CHUANG TZU. *The Complete Works of Chuang Tzu,* tr. by Burton Watson. New York: Columbia University Press, 1968.

I ching. The I Ching or Book of Changes, tr. by Cary F. Baynes. 2 vols. New York: Pantheon Books, 1950.

LAO TZU. *Tao Teh Ching,* tr. by John C. H. Wu. New York: St. John's University Press, 1961.

Li chi. The Li Ki, tr. by James Legge. 2 vols. Oxford: Clarendon Press, 1895.

MENCIUS. *The Works of Mencius,* tr. by James Legge. *The Chinese Classics,* vol. II. Oxford: Clarendon Press, 1895.

Shih chi. See under Ssu-ma Ch'ien.

Shih ching. The Book of Songs, tr. by Arthur Waley. London: Allen & Unwin, 1937.

————. *The Confucian Odes,* tr. by Ezra Pound. Cambridge: Harvard University Press, 1954 [New York: New Directions, n.d.].

SSU-MA CH'IEN. *Shih chi* or *Records of the Grand Historian of China,* tr. by Burton Watson. 2 vols. New York: Columbia University Press, 1958.

Index

Index of Tune Titles